TRADITIONAL AMERICAN CRAFTS

TRADITIONA

AMERICAN CRAFTS

by betsey b. creekmore

PUBLISHED BY HEARTHSIDE PRESS INC.

CREDITS

The Art Institute of Chicago, Illinois.

Audubon House, Key West, Florida. A restoration of the Mitchell-Wolfson Family Foundation. Gerald F. Whaley, Co-ordinator.

Bartow-Pell Mansion, Pelham Bay Park, New York. Headquarters of The International Garden Club.

Bedford Museum, Bedford, New York. The Bedford Historical Society. Miss Dorothy H. Hinitt. Photographs by Prudence Brewer Read.

Blount Mansion, Knoxville, Tennessee. The Governor William Blount Mansion Association. Flower arrangements by members of the Knoxville Garden Club. Photographs by John H. Dempster.

Brothers' House, Old Salem, Winston-Salem, North Carolina. Photographs by Thurmond E. Siceloff.

Bybee-Howell House, Sauvie Island, Oregon. Oregon Historical Society. Thomas Vaughan, Director. Photographs courtesy of Brunschwig & Fils.

Campbell-Whittlesey House, Rochester, New York. The Society for the Preservation of Landmarks in Western New York. Johanne Pouliot, Curator.

Colonial Williamsburg, Williamsburg, Virginia. (The Governor's Mansion, George Wythe House) Miss Marguerite Gignilliat, Press Bureau.

Thomas Cooke House, Edgarton, Massachusetts. Duke County Historical Society. Shell wreath by Mrs. Mary A. Edson.

Coolidge Homestead, Plymouth Notch, Vermont. The Calvin Coolidge Memorial Foundation. Mrs. Sally Thompson, Executive Secretary.

Cooper-Hewitt Museum of Design, New York, New York. Smithsonian Institution.

Craighead-Jackson House, Knoxville, Tennessee. The Blount Mansion Association, The Toms Foundation. Flower arrangements by members of Garden Study Club.

DAR Museum, Memorial Continental Hall, Washington, D.C. National Society of the Daughters of the American Revolution. Frank E. Clapthor, Director-Curator. Crewel embroidery by Mrs. Erwin Frees Seimes.

Denver Art Museum, Denver, Colorado. Colonial Rooms co-sponsored by the Denver Chapter of the National Society of the Colonial Dames of America. Imelda G. DeGraw, Curator of Textiles.

Detroit Historical Museum, Detroit, Michigan. Margot P. Pearsall, Curator.

Diplomatic Reception Suite, United States Department of State, (Monroe Room) Washington, D.C. Flower arrangement by Mrs. Georgia S. Vance.

Eunice Ellis, Brecksville, Ohio, for the apple doll. Photograph by Mrs. Paul Koch.

Essex Institute, Salem, Massachusetts. Collection of Negatives of Historical and Architectural Subjects. Mrs. Dorothy D. Lalone.

Fort Acres, Boscawen, New Hampshire. Omer T. Lassonde.

Fountain Elms, Utica, New York. The Munson-Williams-Proctor Institute.

Ulysses S. Grant House, Detroit, Michigan. Detroit Historical Museum. Margot P. Pearsall, Curator, Department of Social History.

Harlow Old Fort House, Plymouth, Massachusetts. Plymouth Antiquarian Society. Miss Roi T. Briggs, Curator.

Low House, Savannah, Georgia. Headquarters of The National Society of the Colonial Dames of America in the State of Georgia.

Pontalba 1850 House, New Orleans, Louisiana. Louisiana State Museum. Miss Peggy Richards, Director.

President's Cottage, White Sulphur Springs, West Virginia. The Greenbrier Hotel. E. Howard Harvey, Director of Marketing.

The Metropolitan Museum of Art, New York, New York.

Museum of Early Southern Decorative Arts, Winston-Salem, North Carolina. Photographs furnished by Brunschwig & Fils.

CREDITS CONTINUED

Nathaniel Russell House, Charleston, South Carolina. Historic Charleston Foundation. Photograph by Louis Schwartz.

The Newark Museum, Newark, New Jersey. Wilmot T. Bartle, Supervisor of Public Relations.

Philadelphia Museum of Art, Philadelphia, Pennsylvania. Mrs. Elsie McGarvey, Curator; Mrs. Anna Horan.

Saconesset Homestead, West Falmouth, Massachusetts. (Ship's Bottom Roof House) A. B. Gifford, Director.

F. Schumacher & Company, New York, New York.

Seward House, Auburn, New York. Mrs. Bruce E. Lewis.

Smith's Clove, Monroe, New York. Old Museum Village of Smith's Clove.

The Smithsonian Institution, Washington, D.C. Richard H. Howland, Chairman, Department of Civil History.

Southern Highland Handicraft Guild, Asheville, North Carolina. Robert Gray, Director.

Stenton Mansion, Philadelphia, Pennsylvania. Administered by the National Society of the Colonial Dames of America in the Commonwealth of Pennsylvania. Mrs. John M. Wright.

Sunnyside, Tarrytown, New York. Sleepy Hollow Restorations. Miss Patricia E. Smith, Cataloguer of Collections.

Tallman House, Janesville, Wisconsin. Rock County Historical Society. Richard P. Hartung, Director.

Adam Thoroughgood House, Norfolk, Virginia. Administered by the Norfolk Museum of Arts and Sciences.

William Trent House, Trenton, New Jersey. The Trent House Association. Flower arrangements by members of the Garden Club of Trenton.

Vance Birthplace, Weaverville, North Carolina. North Carolina Department of Archives and History. Bob Conway, Director.

Walnut Grove Plantation, Spartanburg, South Carolina. Spartanburg County Historical Association. Frank Coleman, Co-Director.

Waterloo Village, Stanhope, New Jersey (Wellington House) Waterloo Village Restoration.

Josiah Wedgwood & Sons, Inc., New York, New York.

Williamsburg Collection at B. Altman & Company, New York, New York.

Winterthur Museum, Delaware. The Henry Francis du Pont Winterthur Museum. Ian M. G. Quimdy, Registrar.

Woodlawn Plantation, Mount Vernon, Virginia. National Trust for Historic Preservation. J. William Bethea, Director of Public Affairs. Flower arrangements by Fort Belvoir Officers' Wives Garden Club.

Special thanks are due Miss Fanny Andrews, Mrs. John Prugh, and Mrs. David Creekmore of the Knoxville and Knox County Public Library System; Mr. David Harkness, Director of Extension Libraries, The University of Tennessee; Mrs. Ernest Newton, of the Judging Committee of the Garden Club of America; Mrs. Arthur Jones, of the Southern Highland Handicraft Guild; Miss Mary A. Weaver, Salem Academy, Winston-Salem, North Carolina; Mrs. Helen DuPuy Bullock of the National Trust for Historic Preservation; Mr. Ross Bender of the National Park Service; Mr. William Postlethwaite of the *Mountain Press*, Gatlinburg, Tennessee; and Miss Betsey Creekmore, for photographs of corn, gourds, carved butter molds, piano vase, and early Christmas ornaments.

CONTENTS

INTRODUCTION

America's first settlers were homesick. Landing on these alien shores in New England, the New Netherlands, the Middle Colonies and the South, they took the materials at hand and from them tried to re-create not only the houses, but also the comforts and the ornaments they had left behind. Each group had a different heritage, and from their divergent backgrounds in the Old World stemmed regional differences that persisted and became American traditions.

After 1664, when the Dutch relinquished Manhattan Island and the rich Hudson River Valley, all the colonies were British. Some were proprietary colonies, owned by individuals or groups of investors, and others were the property of the Crown, but all were required to trade with the mother country; thus colonial styles were set in England. Seventeenth-century ships were so small, and usually so crowded with new settlers and their scanty belongings, that little space could be spared to "luxuries" for the earlier arrivals. But each group brought a piece or two of furniture (usually a chest, packed with essential clothing and tools), and knowledge of the latest fashion in furnishings. In this manner, each European style change eventually found its way to the American colonies, but each style, as it crossed the ocean, "suffered a sea change." Fashion had to be adapted to the conditions of a pioneer society; inevitably, the colonists simplified what they imitated, and in so doing they added a disciplined look that was typically American.

In the late seventeenth and early eighteenth centuries, newly arrived settlers found the coastal area built up and land there at a premium, so they pushed on into virgin territory. Here they encountered the same problems and shortages, and found the same solutions, as had the first colonists along the seaboard. Over and over the story was repeated — in the Piedmont section of the various colonies, in the over-mountain lands, in the Mississippi Valley, the Great Plains and, finally, on the Pacific Coast.

As Boston, Philadelphia, and New York grew into cosmopolitan port cities, the influence of the Orient was early felt. The East India Company brought fabulous silks, lacquered cabinets, and delicately ornamented porcelains to embelish handsome town houses. In the eighteenth and early nineteenth centuries, New England's sea captains entered the China trade; ships sailed east as well as west, to bring back wallpaper, damasks, and fine furniture from France.

Because southern planters shipped their crops directly to England, they had factors in London to sell the tobacco (later, the cotton) and act as purchasing agents. With proceeds from the sale of a cargo, these early-day personal shoppers bought clothing and household furnishings as requested, and sent them back on the ship's return voyage. Baltimore, Williamsburg, and Charleston followed English fashions with actual imports instead of with Colonial copies.

PRESERVING AMERICA'S LANDMARKS

For three hundred years there was little need to preserve the past, for it was constantly being re-created. In the nineteenth century, however, women were alert to the danger that already threatened some historic homes and quick to avert it whenever possible. George Washington's Mount Vernon and Andrew Jackson's Hermitage were saved from destruction by Ladies' Associations.

By the twentieth century, rapid transportation had erased the distance that fostered regional differences. In the name of progress, venerable houses were being sacrificed to make way for office buildings, housing developments, and broad highways, and the visible evidence of America's heritage was rapidly disappearing. House museums came into being, and major restorations, such as Colonial Williamsburg and Old Sturbridge Village, were undertaken. Each time an ancient house or town was rescued from oblivion, there was greater incentive to save another. Associations for the preservation of antiquities were formed in New England and in various states. The National Trust for Historic Preservation became the guardian of many significant homes, while others were owned or administered by the National Society of the Colonial Dames of America. The National Park Service designated National Historic Shrines, Sites, and Landmarks across the nation.

Saving the buildings themselves was not enough. Authentic furnishings needed to be preserved also. To city-bred children who had never seen a cow, *churn* was a meaningless word, and *butter mold* sounded like an unpleasant sort of fungus. House museums could teach history in the easiest possible way, by giving insight into the lives and labors of preceding generations.

As house museums have proliferated, there has been renewed interest in the crafts that decorated them. Some are very much in use today. Some have disappeared entirely, except for a few carefully preserved examples; others still are practiced, but in changed form; still others are in temporary abeyance, waiting to be revived when fashions in home furnishings come round once again to their periods.

Here, then, are some of the crafts that have contributed to the decoration of American homes, from early colonial days through the nineteenth century—they, too, are part of America's cultural heritage.

I EARLY AMERICAN INTERIORS

The earliest settlers in New England lived in crude shelters while they built their permanent homes. Wood was abundant in the primeval forests that surrounded each settlement, and this was the material most used in building. Stone for foundations and huge central chimneys was all too plentiful in an area where the last slow-moving glacier had littered the land with rocks and boulders. Metal, however, was scarce, and tools were precious. Even the names of the implements are unfamiliar today, but the adz, the froe and the pitsaw (along with the broadax and the maul) turned trees into lumber and lumber into square frame houses with steep-pitched roofs.

By comparison with the cramped ships' quarters in which they had crossed the ocean and with the sod shelters in which they first took refuge, the houses the colonists managed to construct were very comfortable. Many were surprisingly large and, by the standards of the period, even luxurious; the British settlers were building with an eye to the future, for they had come to stay.

In 1609, the Dutch had established a fur-trading post near the present site of Albany, New York, and in 1623 they began building the town of Nieuw Amsterdam on Manhattan Island. Clay was available for brick making, and the high gabled walls of the houses were laid in the ornamental pattern called Flemish bond. On Long Island and in northern New Jersey, settlers from the Lowlands sometimes cut the soft brown native stone in blocks, laying them like brick for the outer walls of gambrel-roofed farmhouses.

In the Middle Colonies, rectangular frame houses were elongated, with a chimney at each end. Brick buildings soon lined the streets of seacoast cities, and large stone farmhouses dotted the countryside.

In the South, where from the beginning of settlement in 1607 the economy had been based on agriculture, large plantations were towns in microcosm. The original rectangular "great house," built of brick or frame, often grew wings when it needed to be enlarged. It was surrounded on three sides by smaller dependencies, each of them a workshop where some necessity was produced, for the plantation was expected to be self-supporting and self-contained. Beyond the shop buildings were barns, tobacco sheds, and the "quarters" for the hands.

It was the Swedish settlers in Delaware who built America's first log cabins. This was the colonial version of a prefabricated house: the trunks of small trees, cut to the same length, were trimmed of branches, and notched at both ends; a few were cut short, to allow for door and window openings. Once this was done, the logs could be quickly fitted together, one atop another, in a square and the cracks between them chinked with clay. Seeing the Swedes build with such relative ease and speed, other settlers moving west put up the same sort of small, crude house, and the log cabin became the trademark of the American frontier.

In western Pennsylvania, the first German settlers built log houses of a different kind. They squared huge timbers and fitted them together with mortised corners. "Cat-and-clay" was the descriptive title for the mortar used: a binder of animal hair kept the clay from crumbling each time it rained. The foot-thick walls of these permanent homes were plastered or paneled inside when time permitted; from a single large room, they grew to two rooms connected by an open passageway called a "dog-trot." Then a second room was added on each side, and the roof was raised to permit a second story; finally, the house was faced with clapboard, brick, or stone.

All the colonists used shake-shingles for the roofs of their houses. Pin oak logs were split and quartered with a wedge and a heavy wooden maul, split again into eighths with a froe, and rived into two-foot shakes. Everyone believed that shingles laid in the dark of the moon would not curl as they dried.

Slab doors were hung on hand-carved wooden hinges, and secured at night with heavy hewn wooden bars; instead of handles, latchstrings of deerhide or leather thongs were used. Small window openings provided not enough light but too much ventilation. Imported glass was extremely scarce and heavily taxed, and although the first industry on the American continent was a glass factory established in 1608 at Jamestown, Virginia, good quality window panes were neither cheap nor plentiful until after the Revolutionary War. The first arrivals in New England advised their followers to bring translucent oiled paper to "cover the openings against the cold." In the majority of houses, windows were merely fitted with outside shutters that were tightly closed and securely latched at night; in more pretentious homes, hinged shutters were installed inside the windows for greater convenience. The outer house walls were thick, and window sills were broad enough to become window seats.

At first, most interior walls were sheathed with rough vertical boards. Even when planking was replaced by paneling, the dull brown of so much wood was rather depressing. Paint was, of course, the first thought (as a preservative as well as for decoration) but paint was considered a luxury, and very little was imported.

COLOR-WASHED WALLS To relieve the monotony of wood and to make small-windowed rooms seem lighter, the colonists began to coat interior walls with plaster made of crushed oyster shells, sand, and sea water. To improve its dusty beige color, they coated it with whitewash made by slaking quicklime in water;

1. *As people continually moved westward into wilderness areas, the houses of the first settlers along the seacoast were copied again and again. The Zebulon B. Vance Birthplace was built in 1795, in the mountains of western North Carolina. In the kitchen (opposite) pine logs of walls and rafters still show the marks of the adz that squared them. The ten-foot fireplace and massive chimney are of handsome brick. The sturdy deal table, the ladder-backed, split-bottomed chairs, and the primitive lighting fixture all are homemade, as are the hanging basket and the wooden dough trays. Dried herbs and hot-peppers for seasonings hang above the fireplace; a flax wheel is beside it, on the right.*

shortly thereafter, they learned to add color with vegetable dyes. Inland colonists developed another kind of wash that worked equally well on plaster or on wood, a primitive ancestor of casein paint. They began with thick, stale buttermilk or clabber from which the whey had been strained off. Into it they beat small amounts of vegetable dye, and to this emulsion they added sifted river sand for body and diffusion.

Still, color washes were only a makeshift, and a poor substitute for oil paints. As soon as they had time, the settlers began to press linseed oil from the flax that was widely grown for linen clothing. Then they learned from the Indians that oil could be extracted from black walnut meats, and found this an excellent vehicle for paints. Pigments were derived by the Indians from natural earths (burnt urber, yellow ochre, red clay) and the settlers added colors obtained from minerals (copperas, verdigris, orpiment, and red and white lead) and from plants (indigo and archil). Although the range was limited, color-starved colonial housewives welcomed these paints and embarked at once on programs of interior decoration.

GRAINING AND MARBLEIZING

The Dutch settlers, who loved color and ornamentation and who were skillful painters, were adept at graining, a process that transformed common deal into a reasonable facsimile of more valuable wood. Not only in the Hudson Valley, but also throughout the colonies, it became the fashion to grain pine paneling in imitation of walnut or mahogany. This was done by painting the entire surface of the pine in a color that matched the lightest tone of the wood to be copied, then applying paint the color of the dark lines in the figuration in streaks with a piece of tow cloth or a stubby, coarse-bristled brush. To obtain a good imitation, it was necessary to have a piece of real walnut or mahogany as a model and to copy the pattern of its grain exactly in paint of precisely the right shade. The completed graining was protected with one or more coats of clear varnish.

Wood also masqueraded as marble, which was too heavy to be imported in large amounts and which was not quarried in quantity until after the Revolution. Here again, the color and veining were copied from an actual sample. The basic white, gray, black, or travertine red color and smooth texture were achieved with several coats of paint; then the black, white, or tan veining was applied with the tip of a large stiff feather, dipped in paint and wobbled across the surface. A final coat of clear shellac or varnish completed the illusion.

STIPPLING AND MOTTLING

Graining and marbleizing were difficult to do well and expensive to have done by professionals. So great was the fad for "glazed" woodwork that other, less difficult, techniques were developed and came into very common use. Stippling required little artistic ability but was very effective. Painted wood was given a top coat of a lighter or darker shade; while this paint was wet, it was jabbed with a large, coarse-bristled brush. Each bristle removed a minute quantity of the wet paint, allowing the color of the undercoat to show through in an allover pattern of tiny dots.

A quicker and even easier method was mottling, which also was done on a top coat of wet paint different in color from the layer underneath. The painter blotched the surface with a pad of tow cloth or a large cork, removing some but not all the wet paint from each mark, and thus exposing

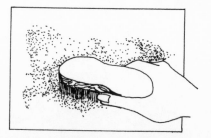
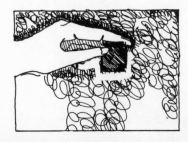

2. In 1927, Henry Francis du Pont began to enlarge the family residence, Winterthur, to accommodate his unparalleled collection of beautiful and unusual American rooms. The Fractur Room, (opposite) originally part of a Bucks County, Pennsylvania, farmhouse retains the first coat of mottled blue paint on its fireplace and window paneling. The large open volume on the walnut center table is the Book of Martyrs, printed at the Ephrata Cloisters in 1748; around it are illuminated hymnals and exercise books. The dower chests repeat in paint the motifs developed over many centuries for Fractur work.

the undercoat. In either method, a glaze of clear varnish was added, to protect the decorative work and to give the high sheen that was considered very desirable.

GLAZING WITH BUTTERMILK
A streaky white-on-color glaze was easiest of all to obtain; plain buttermilk was brushed over colored oil paint. It did not adhere thoroughly to the smooth surface, and therefore did not cover completely but dried in raised, chalky lines. It was then covered with varnish; had it not been covered in this way, it soon would have flaked away.

By the end of the seventeenth century, fine white plaster was being made of crushed limestone rock, sifted sand, and water; for greater strength, horsehair often was added as a binder.

PAINTING PLASTER
It was fashionable to combine paneling and plaster on the same wall. At first, wainscoting of natural or grained wood extended far up the wall, with a wide strip of plaster above. In the eighteenth century more plaster and less wood was used; a paneled dado, ending in a chair rail, covered only the lower three or four feet, and above it the wall was plastered up to a wide wooden cornice. This in turn was surmounted by a plaster ceiling. It was customary to panel the entire fireplace wall of such a room, and special emphasis was given to the chimney breast. Sometimes the wooden wainscot and cornice were painted in a dark shade to contrast with light-colored plaster.

Simulated Wood
Plaster was sometimes grooved and painted to resemble wood. Vertical "paneling" was outlined with the point of a putty knife on a wet plaster wall; when dry, the plaster was painted, and wood grain was simulated by streaking the surface of the paint with a stiff feather.

Molded Plaster
By the late eighteenth century, molded plaster had become a decorative medium. Skilled workmen cast segments of an elaborate design in a series of molds, fitting these pieces together on a still wet plaster wall or ceiling. Usually the background and the relief work were painted the same color, but sometimes the raised decoration was white against a pastel wall. Occasionally, important motifs were picked out or highlighted with gilding.

At this time, rococo *boiserie* was imitated with carved wooded molding glued on plaster walls; often the areas outlined with molding were painted white while the background plaster was given a pastel tint.

DECORATIVE PAINTING ON PLASTER
Colonists whose purses would not stretch to wallpaper (which was available early in the eighteenth century, but was extremely expensive) found it possible to achieve fashionably patterned walls with paint. In one method, plaster was first painted or whitewashed in white or a pale pastel shade. Then, in a darker color, stenciled motifs and borders were applied. Usually such designs were delicate and stylized, and quite widely spaced. The overall pattern repeated at measured intervals a design made up of composite stencils; the continuous border was painted with a one-piece stencil, scrolled or geometric in character.

Murals
Another method, which required the services of a professional artist or of a talented family member, was the painting of murals on plastered walls in emulation of French scenic wallpaper. The drawing room, the dining room, or the hall might be chosen to receive such decorations, which usually were landscapes. Itinerant painters, armed with stencils and sketchbooks of mural designs, travelled through the colonies; they found the Hudson River Valley an area especially receptive to their talents.

3. *Several rooms from the Palladian-style Russell House, built in Rhode Island in 1772, are preserved and displayed at the Denver Art Museum, joint sponsor with the National Society of the Colonial Dames of America. The walls show composite stenciling used to add color and pattern to plain white plaster. On the floor is a small hooked rug in a geometric design typical of the early eighteenth century. Painted chairs, stenciled in color and lined in gold, were much admired in the United States during the belated Classic Revival, after 1800.*

Flocked Plaster

In the most elegant homes, the drawing room walls (above a painted, paneled dado) were covered in the eighteenth century with heavy patterned demask. Only the wealthy could afford to hang their walls with imported crimson, emerald green, or golden yellow silk, but the rich effect was much admired and soon imitated in a process called flocking. Designs drawn or stenciled on a painted plaster wall were coated with glue; then fine chopped dyed wool was pressed into the glue to form a colorful raised pattern that looked not unlike cut velvet. Today's moiré, damask, and flocked wallpapers strive for the look of silk hangings and flocked plaster.

STENCILED FLOORS

In most colonial homes, the floors were made of soft pine, which was easy to split into planking but which splintered badly as it wore. It was therefore customary to seal pine floors with several coats of paint of a dark color that harmonized well with the lighter tone of the walls.

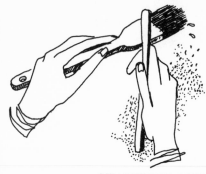

In the Hudson River Valley, where the Dutch love of elaborate ornamentation persisted long after Nieuw Amsterdam had become New York, painted floors often received further decoration in the form of stenciled patterns. The solid color surface (brick red, dull green, vermilion, or mustard yellow) was carefully measured and marked off, and repeated pattern in a darker color was applied with one-piece stencils that usually were cut in small geometric figures. The effect was rather like mosaic or decorated tile.

SPATTERDASH PAINTING

In New England and the Middle Colonies, rough board floors were more often smoothed and brightened by giving them several coats of black or dark green paint and splattering its surface with one or more light colors. This was done by holding a full paintbrush horizontal, at arm's length, and striking its handle sharply with a stick to make droplets of paint fly off in all directions. Spatterdash linoleum patterns of today imitate these colorful and practical colonial floors.

FLOOR CLOTHS

During the eighteenth century, wooden kitchen floors were protected with a type of covering that could be called the forerunner of linoleum and asphalt tile: the floor cloth. Canvas or sailcloth was stretched over the entire floor and tacked in place above a padding of straw. Then the cloth was given several coats of oil paint to make it waterproof and durable underfoot; the final coat was applied in a decorative design. Sometimes the surface was laid off in squares and painted in alternating light and dark colors, like a gigantic chessboard. Sometimes paint was wiped on and veined, in imitation of granite, slate, or marble. Occasionally a repeated geometric pattern was stenciled on, or a picture was painted freehand. Because they were of perishable material and received hard usage, floor cloths wore out quickly and had to be replaced frequently. Only a few complete examples still exist.

KITCHENS IN AMERICAN HISTORY

The Seventeenth-Century Kitchen

The kitchen was the heart of the seventeenth-century home. In fact, it often comprised the entire house of an artisan or a small farmer, except for an unheated sleeping loft above it that was reached by a ladder. Here the family not only cooked and ate but worked and, in many cases, slept. One wall of the room was given over to the gaping fireplace and its accoutrements that included an oven built into the chimney at waist height, a kettle suspended over the flames, and a spider—a long-handled iron skillet on three legs that raised it over the glowing coals. A wooden settle, placed at right angles to the hearth, had a high solid back to give protection from drafts; on the opposite side of the fireplace was the inevitable cradle. In the center of the floor stood a long, narrow trestle or sawbuck table flanked by backless benches, with a chair at one end for the master of the house. In a far corner, there usually was a bed raised so high off the floor that a stepstool was necessary for climbing in and out of it; there was also a trundle bed, a low box-like affair on wooden wheels, that was pushed under the tall bedstead when not in use. Chests that held linens and clothing were ranged against the walls, and in one corner there was sure to be a spinning wheel.

Wooden trenchers were the only plates in everyday use, and serving platters were of wood or pewter. This was true not only in the provinces but in England—as late as 1713, Joseph Addison would describe china cups and plates as "playthings for women of all ages." The few cherished pieces of Chinese porcelain or delft pottery that survived the sea voyage were displayed in press cupboards or on plate racks, and graced the table only on state occasions.

Trenchers usually were rectangular slabs of wood, scooped out to a shallow depression with a raised rim; two people shared each trencher, which was cleaned after the meal by scouring it with sand. Wooden mugs and wooden or clamshell spoons, plus hunting knives, completed the table setting. A mug was whittled and scrapped from a single block of wood; its outer surface was sanded and polished with beeswax or, more rarely, was ornamented with carving.

Seventeenth century housewives treasured horn drinking cups, considering them a great improvement over wooden mugs. These were made of the inner layer of deer or ox horns which, when dried and polished, looked remarkably like tortoise shell. The horns were naturally hollow but were not always flat at the base; to make them stand steady, they were mounted on pewter and finished at the lip with a matching rim of the metal. In the homes of the affluent, horn cups were based and rimmed with silver.

Powder horns hung on the wall as decorations when not in use. Often they were highly ornamental, for it was the custom to carve as well as to polish them. Animals were logically the favorite motifs, but powder horns also were carved with maps, landscapes, portraits, and even (paper often being unobtainable) with deeds or family records.

Although meat sometimes was roasted over the coals (on a spit turned by child power), most cooking took the form of soups and stews. In the absence of forks, "spoon meat" was easiest to eat. America's forests were full of small game and the waters teemed with fish, but gunpowder, shot, and fishhooks were in very short supply and once expended could not be replaced. Maize was destined to become the mainstay of the settlers' diet.

In the eighteenth century, the increasing availability of metals brought *Eighteenth-Century* "conveniences" to the kitchen: half-round roasting ovens that faced the *Kitchens* fire and cooked meat on all sides at once by reflecting heat; candle molds that did away with the tedious dipping of wicks in melted tallow; long-handled forks and ladles to take the place of those made of wood or gourd. Glass bottles replaced gourd flasks. The bedstead and the trundle bed left the corner of the kitchen and moved with the clothes chest to a bedroom. The dining room became an entity, and treen ware was no longer set on the guest table. Pewter plates and tankards, two-tined forks, and molded pewter spoons were for everyday use; china plates and silver spoons appeared when company came to dinner. Prosperity was epitomized by the serving of tea, in thin handleless china cups, in a drawing room furnished with upholstered sofas and chairs, tall secretaries, and delicate small tables. The kitchen remained the workshop, and the craft center of the home, throughout the colonial period and into the nineteenth century.

In the South, the kitchen was relegated very early to a small outbuild- *The Summer Kitchen* ing; often it was the one-room cabin in which the architect had lived while the "great house" was under construction. The obvious reason for the separate kitchen was that it lessened the ever-present danger of fire. It also, however, kept the family's living quarters cooler in summer and free of cooking odors the year around. Servants carried the food (on covered trays or in dishes kept hot by a base compartment that held boiling water) from the kitchen building to the dining room in the main house. In New England and the Middle Colonies, many houses had detached "summer kitchens" that were used only in hot weather.

Restored Kitchens in Historic Houses   Visitors to house museums like to linger in restored kitchens, for there the wide gulf that separates life in the twentieth century from life in colonial days is instantly apparent. A horn cup, a gourd bowl, a massive kettle swinging at the end of a crane, are visible proof of the ingenuity and the strength of early Americans. The stark simplicity of the room itself is a surprise: brown floor, walls, ceiling, and furniture; gray stone chimney breast, gray pewter plates and slavers; black wrought-iron utensils. Eyes are irresistibly drawn to a heap of colorful ornamental gourds in a basket, to the cluster of multicolored ears of corn with turned-back yellow shucks, and to the glowing string of red peppers hanging by the fireplace—mute evidence of the importance of color in colonial homes.

4.   The kitchen of the Russell House displays (left) a clock reel, with exposed mechanism, for measuring spun thread into "knots." The two wooden paddles on the chair beside it are covered with metal teeth; they were used to card wool. Across the room is a small flax wheel with foot treadle. On the floor is a braided rag rug; dyed cloth strips make up the solid center and decorative bands, while untreated rags produced random color. The tin lantern has a pierced sunburst pattern.

II DECORATIVE PAINTING AND STENCILING

All very early American houses were sparsely furnished with pieces almost invariably homemade. The first Englishmen in New England made "memory furniture" in the Jacobean fashion: heavy oak chests, tables, press cupboards, and settees. Chairs were remarkably uncomfortable, with unpadded seats and knobbed banister backs. They were reserved for adult use; children sat on backless forms or on low, three-legged stools.

In the Middle Colonies and the South, the first furniture was extremely plain and functional. Settlers who had only axes, saws, and knives to work with naturally chose woods that would be easy to chop and split, and neither nail nor glue was needed to put simple pieces together. The bulged peg of a dried hickory chair rung would be driven into a slightly smaller hole in a leg of green maple or oak; as the green wood dried, it gripped the peg ever tighter in an almost unbreakable bond.

Of course, furniture made of fine-grained wood with a rich natural hue—black walnut, maple, or wild cherry—remained untreated except for frequent rubbing with linseed oil to enhance its sheen. Oak, heavy and stark when plain, lent itself well to carving and was most often ornamented in this way. However, chests and chairs of sturdy but unprepossessing poplar, hickory, or pine were usually painted, stained, or grained to make them more attractive.

In many early pieces, several different woods (perhaps the leftovers from other furniture-making projects) were combined. Paint disguised dissimilar materials as it added desirable color. During the eighteenth century, throughout the northeastern colonies, dark green was a favorite paint color for Windsor chairs with their curved backs of slender spindles.

By the time the Queen Anne style reached these shores, colonial master builders were constructing handsome houses, and cabinetmakers were creating fine furniture from native hardwoods. Life was easier, at least in the seaboard cities, and better roads made possible the shipment of manufactured articles not just from one town to the next but also from one colony to another. The result was that pretentious eighteenth-century American homes reflected both the fashion and the comfort of England.

The children of Germans who arrived in America in the early 1700's learned from their parents an art that would be handed down and practiced in Pennsylvania until the middle of the nineteenth century. This was the process of pen and brush illumination called *Fractur;* it had been nurtured and venerated in the Rhine Valley since medieval times.

Fractur painting originated in monasteries during the Middle Ages, where it was done by monks to ornament the pages of a missal or a

5. *Fractur, the medieval art of manuscript illumination that was practiced in Pennsylvania until the mid-nineteenth century, combined decorative lettering with stenciled motifs. This certificate in the collection of the Newark Museum attests the birth on January 10, 1805, of a daughter, Nancy, to William Loeffler and his wife, Maria. Lettering, stippling, and crosshatching were done with a quill pen, and color was washed on with tiny brushes made of cat hair.*

breviary. In Pennsylvania, it was employed at first to illustrate church hymnals and decorate their title pages. From hymnals and religious books of all kinds, its use spread to small manuscript songbooks made for music schools, to school awards, to baptismal and marriage certificates that were framed and hung on the wall, and finally to pictures especially made for wall decoration.

The colored inks for Fractur painting were vegetable and mineral pigments dissolved in alcohol. They were applied with quill pens and with tiny brushes made of cat hair, and the finished paintings were protected with a varnish made from the gum of the wild cherry tree. The colors were vivid, and often most artistically combined. In the religious community at Ephrata, where some of the best illuminating was done, the penwork was minute and marvelously intricate; German script was lettered with exquisite care, and borders and motifs were stippled or crosshatched before being colored with ink. The brushwork was as delicate and precise as in a Japanese painting.

These German Protestants had come to America as refugees, in groups that were sometimes whole church congregations. The motifs they employed in illuminating had religious significance, and the symbols were as old as Fractur painting itself. The three-petaled tulip, which appeared in almost every illustration, represented the Trinity; the dove had a dual meaning: Peace and Baptism into the household of Faith; the heart signified Christian charity. Often these and other symbols were combined in a stylized tree of life.

In William Penn's tolerant colony, the sacred symbols persisted, but as the use of Fractur techniques was extended to baptismal certificates, school awards and secular paintings, old motifs were altered and new ones were added. Stiff human figures—queer little boys in knee-breeches and round hats, and quaint little girls in wide skirts and striped aprons—replaced angels. The dove sprouted a topknot, a long curving tail, and brilliant plumage, and turned into a parrot. Other flowers (daisies and thistles from the Old World, dogwood blossoms from the New) joined the tulip, but never superseded it.

Schoolmasters taught the art of Fractur painting to their pupils, using plant dyes thinned with whisky and paper stencils, and the idea of stenciled decorations carried over into Pennsylvania homes.

By 1740, the Pennsylvania Dutch (who were *not* Dutch, but German) were using stencils to add colorful designs to painted dower chests, bride's boxes, chair rails, and settee backs. The motifs were borrowed, as was the technique, from Fractur work, but paint with a base of walnut oil was used instead of ink, stencils were cruder, and colors were harsher.

To her new home, each bride took a dower chest, filled with linens and bedding made by and for her during her girlhood. The chest itself, a large and sturdy wooden box with a hinged lid and raised panels on front and sides, was painted a bright solid color and its panels were given a background of a light contrasting shade. Each panel was further ornamented with stenciled motifs. Above all things, the Pennsylvania Germans admired symmetry. The two halves of their stenciled designs were mirror images of each other; if there was a blue-and-green dove facing right, there was sure to be another facing left. Instead of cutting separate stencils for two such birds, the decorator used one stencil twice—by turning it over—and this insured that the second dove would be exactly like the first one, in reverse.

A bride's box was a small container for personal treasures: ribbons, laces, buttons, and bits of jewelry. In construction it was a smaller, finer version of a cheese box; the sides were made of very thin wood, soaked in water and bent into a round or oval shape, and the removable lid was finished with a lapped rim (a single narrow strip) that fitted down snugly over the upper edge. The bride herself was expected to line the box with padded cloth, and to paint the exterior (usually in cream color) and ornament the top and sides with stenciled motifs or freehand decorations.

The descendants of early Dutch settlers in the Hudson Valley were so enamored of decorative painting that a room with murals on the walls and geometric stenciling on the floor might also have a painted landscape on an overmantel panel and a painted fireboard that covered the fireplace when it was not in use. Much of this work was done by journeyman painters,

STENCILED FURNITURE

Pennsylvania Dutch Design

but then, as now, artistically inclined housewives enjoyed making their own decorations.

A *kas* might glow with the colors of Holland's favorite motifs: floral garlands, plump cherubs, ribbon bowknots and streamers. Chests and chairs were given bright backgrounds with stenciling superimposed; vines and flowers were added freehand. All this was ladies' work, and they applied their oil paints not only with brushes but also with corks and feathers.

New England Designs   In Connecticut, the famous Guilford and Hadley chests were paneled and painted in a manner very similar to that of German dower chests. The stencils, however, were reminiscent of England and Scotland with their rose and thistle motifs.

After 1700, in Connecticut and Massachusetts, the press cupboard beloved of seventeenth-century housewives was replaced by built-in cupboards

6. *The Metropolitan Museum of Art, in New York City, has so many general and specialized collections that a lifetime could be spent in exploring and studying them. From the American Wing comes the exhibit (opposite) of Pennsylvania German furniture and decorations of the eighteenth and nineteenth centuries. Framed Fractur paintings are grouped above painted and stenciled dower chests that borrowed motifs from the medieval art of manuscript illumination. On the table is a typical oval bride's box of thin painted wood, ornamented with stenciling and freehand painting. The small wooden candle chest at left shows the American dogwood motif that was popular but did not supplant the three-petalled tulip, which is used on the dower chest below. Even the slipware made in Pennsylvania derived its symmetrical decorative designs from Fractur work.*

7. *In the Pennsylvania German Bedroom (below) at Winterthur Museum, the green painted chest, dated 1834, has delicate and beautiful stenciling around its edges. Each drawer is centered with a symmetrical stenciled design of birds and small flowers; the same composite stencils have been used on every drawer, but from them four quite different compositions have been made. Over the fireplace (fitted with a Franklin stove and Hessian andirons), the carved wooden overmantel frames a balanced design of flowers and leaves in three pitchers, painted on the plaster. The framed painting on the left wall is the Peaceable Kingdom by a Bucks County Quaker artist, Edward Hicks. A large, bright hooked rug has magnified versions of the flower motifs used in crewel embroidery and on stenciled furniture. The tall-painted Windsor chair on the right is lined with gilding.*

in corners or in the fireplace wall. These retained the earlier concept of open display shelves above a closed storage space, but their tops curved outward in a carved design that usually resembled a giant scallop shell. The interior of the open cupboard often was painted dark red, vermilion, or light green, and against such a colorful background a shelf display of delft or Chinese porcelain showed to perfection.

In the early nineteenth century, the "fancy chair" adapted by Hitchcock from Sheraton's classic revival design was adopted by New Englanders and made peculiarly their own. After the chair was painted in a solid color (black was favored, but green, red, brown and gray were sometimes seen) a design was stenciled in color or in gilt on the rather wide top slat. Smaller linear stencils were used on rungs, legs, and side pieces, and arabesques were often added, freehand. Beginning with these Empire side chairs, the vogue for stenciled decorations was extended to regional pieces: deacon's benches, Boston rockers, even buggy seats, were painted, stenciled in color, and touched with gilding.

STENCILS   By definition, a stencil is "a thin sheet of metal, wood, cardboard, parchment, or architect's linen with a cut out pattern." When a stencil is laid flat and brushed with paint or ink, its pattern is reproduced on the surface

8. *At the Newark Museum is this cane-seated "fancy chair" made between 1820 and 1835 and attributed to David Alling. It is painted charcoal black with reddish streaks and is decorated with parcel gilt. The wider center slat, typical of Classic Revival chairs in New Jersey and the Hudson Valley, is shaped and stenciled to represent twin cornucopias filled with harvest fruits and melons. The central cluster of plume-shaped leaves supports a circular medallion with a tiny stenciled repeat of fruit in a footed bowl. The gilt stencils on the back posts suggest the delicate inlays of wood or mother-of-pearl seen on fine Hepplewhite and Sheraton-style pieces.*

underneath it. Making a stencil can be as simple as cutting one hole in a piece of paper; it can also be extremely complicated, and a dozen or more stencils may be required to complete a single design.

In colonial days, stencils made of thin wood or sheet tin were available where paint was sold. Women who did not have access to city shops (and those who liked to exercise their artistic talents) made their own. They began by tacking a sheet of parchment or stiffly starched linen to a board, and drawing or tracing a design in ink. The outline was cut with the sharp tip of a penknife, and carefully trimmed with scissors.

Composite Stencils

Most early American stencils (with the exception of the geometric patterns used on floors) were composite designs. The fruit-basket motif that was universally popular throughout the colonies required a basket stencil plus smaller cutouts of an apple, a pear, a bunch of grapes, and leaves of various shapes and sizes. Creating a design from these separate pieces was rather like making an arrangement of fresh fruits. The artist began with the basket and added the fruit, piece by piece, until the effect was pleasingly balanced; the small stencils were allowed to overlap, and to overhang the lip of the container. This took time, for each portion of the composition had to dry thoroughly before the next could be added.

Actually, these early decorations were a combination of stenciling and freehand drawing. Painting over a stencil gave only a solid background; color shading and such details as veining on leaves had to be added later. For example, a bunch-of-grapes stencil was a mere edge-outline. The individual grapes had to be shaped, shaded, and highlighted with a brush, and tendrils were drawn in with a feather.

One-piece Stencils

After 1800, one-piece stencils became increasingly popular. It was much easier, of course, to paint an entire pattern at one fell swoop than to build a design gradually from component parts. During the Federal period, the American eagle had come to symbolize the power and pride of the young Republic; the curving outspread wings, the tiered feathers, and the fierce and fearless head could all be reproduced at once from a single intricate stencil. An arrangement of fruit could be outlined complete instead of piece by piece. A narrow garland of flowers and leaves could be stenciled with a single sweep of the paint brush. To purists who had enjoyed using composite stencils with imagination and artistry, this was like reading Caesar with a pony!

The one-piece stencil was easily distinguishable because there were definite blank spaces (called "bridges") surrounding each unit of the design. No matter how many tendrils and scrolls were added freehand, the effect was stiff and prĕcise; as the Victorian era continued, this very precision came to be accounted a virtue.

PAINTED TINWARE (TOLE)

Even in New York, not every colonial home had painted furniture, but any object made of tin—trays, tea caddies, boxes, pitchers, coffeepots— was sure to be painted and apt to be stenciled. A few beautifully lacquered cabinets and trays found their way from the Orient to Boston and Philadelphia, where they were treasured and greatly admired, but the craze for painting tinware was imported from England along with the materials for the craft. In the early eighteenth century, leisured English ladies fell to decorating lacquered trays with freehand painting and with stencils; the process was called *japanning,* for the finest oriental vegetable lacquer was produced in Japan by careful refining of the sap of a tree called *Rhus verniciflua*. Chinese designs were delicately beautiful and far more plentiful, but the finishes were of inferior quality. By 1740, lacquers, camel's-hair brushes, and bronzing powders were for sale in the large eastern port cities, and southern planters were writing, at the behest of their wives, to their London factors for "materials to be used in japanning."

Japanning Trays   A large round, oval, or rectangular tray that could be prominently displayed in the dining room when not in use was the favorite piece of tinware for japanning. Black was the usual background color, although dark green and dark red were also popular. Three coats of thick lacquer were applied; after each coat, the thick paint required several days to dry. In the center of the tray a stenciled arrangement of flowers or a pastoral scene often was used instead of the ubiquitous fruit basket. In any case, after the design had been outlined with stencils and filled in with a brush, it was shaded with bronzing powder. This was done when the paint was almost dry; a pad of velvet was dipped into the gold powder and wiped across the slightly sticky surface. Then some of the powder was removed by rubbing over it with a clean bit of velvet wrapped around the fingers. The edges of the tray were lined in gold by applying bronzing powder with a very thin, pointed brush.

Hardly had colonial ladies mastered this technique when word arrived from England that such painted trays were no longer in style. Stenciling must be done on a bronzed or a tortoise-shell background.

Bronzing sounded easier, so most ladies tried it first. After the tray had been given two coats of black lacquer, a third coat was added and allowed to become almost dry. Beginning at the center, pale-gold bronzing powder was polished into the surface with a circular motion, using a velvet pad or a scrap of fur. Working toward the edges, deeper shades of bronzing powder were used: dark gold for the middle background, and deep copper for the edges. When the surface was completely dry, the excess powder was washed off. Then colored stenciling was added, and high-lighted with gold powder.

Tortoise-shell decoration was actually much less difficult. It also began with three coats of black lacquer, all thoroughly dry; then irregularly shaped blotches of vermilion paint were scattered over the surface and allowed to dry for twenty-four hours. Gray lacquer was brushed over the vermilion; while it was still wet, it was wiped off with a soft cloth. This removed some of the vermilion and streaked the rest, and the tray was ready for lining and stenciling. The combination of black, vermilion, and gray lacquers had produced a mottled brown.

By the same methods tin tea caddies, pitchers, coffeepots and boxes were stenciled in smaller designs. The craft is still practiced in much the same manner, except that modern materials are easier to us. To simulate colonial tortoise-shell finish, a mixture of one-third clear varnish and two-thirds asphaltum varnish is substituted for gray lacquer. For bronzing, shading, and lining, new metallic finishes that are packaged in small tubes can be wiped or brushed onto a completely dry surface; they come with complete instructions for their use. Finishes, varnishes, and one-piece cardboard or plastic stencils in traditional designs are available where artist's supplies are sold.

Stenciling a Tray

An acceptable replacement for the thick black lacquer of colonial times is made by stirring one tablespoonful of clear varnish into a half pint of flat black enamel. It may be used not only on tinware, but also on aluminum, wood, plastic, or papier-mâché. This paint is applied in a thick layer, with long even strokes of a full brush, to leave no lap or bristle marks. After drying for twenty-four hours, the surface should be lightly sanded and wiped clean with a damp cloth. A second and a third paint coat, at twenty-four hour intervals, will prepare the surface of a tray for decorating.

In using a rectangular one-piece stencil with a cutout fruit-basket design, center the stencil exactly on the flat surface of the tray by careful measurement. Outline its corners with a pointed piece of chalk, and secure the stencil in position with masking tape, which is easily removed and leaves no sticky residue on a painted surface. Brush over the stencil with background color—preferably dull yellow or beige—to obtain a complete edge-outline; to be sure the paint has penetrated all small slits, turn the brush on edge and go over them a second time. Remove the stencil at once, lifting it straight up

9.   *This exquisite lace-edged tole tray is from the collection of the Winterthur Museum. Against a tortoise-shell background, the delicate tracery of a rococo border and an asymmetrical pastoral scene in the late-eighteenth-century French manner combine composite stenciling with freehand painting. Stencils were edge outlines only, to be detailed and shaded with a brush; here the foliage and the rams' heads are so cleverly altered by placement and brushwork that they do not appear stylized.*

by its edges in order not to smudge the pattern. Remove any paint that has run beyond the edge with a bit of cloth wrapped over a fingernail. If a clear outline has not been obtained, wait until the paint has dried and then recenter the stencil in its corner chalk marks, tape it down, and paint again. Allow the background color to dry thoroughly, and wipe away the chalk markings with a dampened cloth. Using artist's oils and small brushes, color the various elements of the design beginning with the bas-

10.   *The death of George Washington in 1799 was followed by a wave of "memorial crafts"—commemorative paintings on velvet, china, silk, and metal were made from stencils sold with the materials for their use. This rectangular tray with cutout handles has a stenciled border of leaves and flowers; veining, stippling of the flower centers and dashes were added freehand. The central medallion, a portrait bust of Washington, has allegorical significance. The hovering angel is awarding him a victor's crown, and the words PRO PATRIA are from the Latin* Dulce et decorum est pro patria mori *(Sweet and fitting it is to die for one's own country). The tray is from the collection of The Art Institute of Chicago.*

ket. Indicate inner outlines where the various pieces of fruit overlap. When this paint has dried, brush on color shading, and add veining and tendrils freehand with a very small pointed brush. Apply gold shading and highlights with a fingertip; then line the edge of the tray with a brush dipped in tube-gold, using a ruler as a guide.

After stenciling, apply clear varnish to seal and protect the design. One coat will suffice if the tray is intended only for display; three coats, each lightly sanded before another is applied, will protect the surface for ordinary usage. As the final step, give the tray a light coat of white liquid wax which dries clear but dull, and buff to a matte.

CHINA PAINTING

After the Industrial Revolution, painted tole was mass-produced in such quantities that it was no longer necessary or fashionable to decorate tin by hand. China painting suddenly became the thing to do.

This was considered so useful and ladylike an accomplishment that throughout the nineteenth century it was included in the curriculum of every fashionable finishing school. Mineral colors (in an oil medium) were applied to "blanks" of undecorated white china that were sold in hardware stores. Graphite paper was used to transfer a tracing to the china surface.

The design was then outlined in India ink, which disappeared during the firing process, and painted in three steps: 1) a light coat of background color on each element of the design; 2) shading with a second and perhaps a third color; 3) shadows and final details. Firing could not successfully be done at home, but every town had its brickyard; for a small fee, a dozen dinner plates could be fired at the local brickkiln.

China would not have been decorated at home had inexpensive and attractive tableware been available. The finest dinnerware was still being imported from England, Germany, and especially from France. American manufacturers were producing sturdy pottery and shapely ironstone ware, but no really outstanding thin china; the better amateur efforts at china decorating were superior to the factory product.

As a case in point, when Rutherford B. Hayes became President of the United States in 1877, Mrs. Hayes decided to spend a large part of a congressional appropriation for redecorating the White House on a state dinner service. Theodore R. Davis of New Jersey was commissioned to make a series of water-color paintings, featuring the flora and fauna of North America. Davis' designs were bold and striking, but difficult to reproduce upon porcelain in mineral colors. Although Mrs. Hayes was anxious to have the dinner service a product of the United States from start to finish, no American manufacturer had the necessary equipment and experience for such an undertaking. So the thousand-piece service was made of faïence, at Limoges, France.

In 1889 Mrs. Benjamin Harrison, herself an accomplished china painter, helped to design a new presidential dinner service. Ears of corn were featured motifs, along with the American eagle and forty-three stars representing the states of the Union. Once again the design was typically American but the china was marked *Made in France*. Not until after World War I was a state dinner service made for the White House in the United States: the white and gold Woodrow Wilson china, with service plates bordered in cobalt blue and centered by the Presidential seal, was designed and produced at the Lenox pottery in Trenton, New Jersey.

Of course, not every piece of hand-painted china was for table use. Mustache cups, bowls, vases, pitchers and plaques all bore the favorite Victorian moss rose; thousands of Parian figurines were painted in pastel colors in imitation of imported Dresden. Since these occasional pieces would not be subjected to frequent washing in hot water, they usually were finished with a "glaze" of clear varnish, but were not fired. Repeated coats of very thick paint, applied at twenty-four hour intervals, could build up certain portions of a design for a three-dimensional effect. Flower centers, bowknots and streamers, and the plumage of birds often were emphasized in this way; sometimes raised dots (like French knots) were scattered over an entire vase.

Ceramics Today   Victorian china painters were content to confine their decorative efforts to ready-made blanks and factory-produced Parian vases or figurines, but the safe and relatively easy to operate electric kiln has enabled twentieth century craftsmen to enter and enjoy the wider field of ceramics. With a small home kiln, it is possible to do both biscuit and gloss firing; the temperature for maturing most clays and glazes is 1900° Fahrenheit. Across the nation, ceramists attend classes, form clubs, exchange molds, share kilns, and exhibit handwork that ranges from simple glazed bowls to intricate enamelled designs on copper.

11. *This tall hand-painted vase is one of a pair used at the ends of a square grand piano in the 1850's. The completed design was covered with clear varnish, but was not fired. In the intervening years, gilded dotwork and scrollwork have almost disappeared, but the mineral colors of the flowers and autumn leaves still are fresh and bright.*

12. *Although paintings on velvet were most often framed and glazed, the same techniques were sometimes applied to decorative objects. This nest of three workboxes, handmade of cardboard and covered with velvet, is from the Campbell-Whittlesey House. Each has a different stenciled pattern. The largest and smallest have floral designs, while the top of the middle-size box has the familiar theorem fruit basket, done this time in blue, green, and yellow to correspond with the flowers on the companion pieces.*

Since tasteful, dishwasher-safe dinner services are universally available and comparably inexpensive, most present day painters on china prefer to decorate accessory pieces (such as fruit and flower pyramids, vases, and figurines with overglaze designs which are kilned at a temperature of about 1375°.

Many ceramics enthusiasts begin from scratch by making original press- or drain-molds of plaster. Clays are available (at hobby shops and ceramics centers) in plastic form for modeling, in liquid state for casting, or as powder to be mixed for glazing. For beginners (and for school or scout groups) there are special "clays" that harden without firing. Glazes made for use with these clays harden in the kitchen oven at 150°, but such pieces usually are painted and covered with clear varnish in the nineteenth-century manner. Several types of clays, with companion glazes, are made for oven firing. Articles molded from these are first thoroughly air-dried and then are baked for fifteen minutes at 250°.

Toward the end of the colonial period, decorated window shades were much admired. Designs were drawn freehand or stenciled on thin, translucent cambric, and colored with dyes for an effect of stained glass as the light came through. Some such shades were sold commercially, but many more were made at home, from directions in contemporary art books.

During the nineteenth century, opaque cloth window shades were regarded necessary for privacy. These were made to order in solid colors—usually

PAINTED WINDOW SHADES

dark green or brown—and it was the fashion to add stenciled borders and large repeated motifs to their centers. Much of this stenciled work was very neatly outlined and painted in muted colors, with extra hand detailing that entitled the completed shade to be considered a "work or art," but Victorian painted shades lacked the lighted effect that had distinguished their predecessors.

PAINTING ON VELVET   Early in the nineteenth century, painting on velvet was a popular craft. This was much more difficult than it sounded, and for that reason it was highly esteemed as a form of artistic endeavor. Even those Victorian ladies who could paint realistic roses on a smooth hard china plate or stencil a

13. *The collection of American Primitives at the Newark Museum in New Jersey includes this glistening nineteenth-century still life of flowers and fruits—a tinsel painting on glass. Such a design had first to be outlined in reverse, on the back of the glass; if this was not perfectly done the picture looked very strange when viewed from the other side, so stencils were customarily used. The outline was filled in with colors, and the portions of the motifs to be high-lighted were covered with silver size. Thin silver leaf, or tin foil was pressed over the sizing, to which it adhered immediately, and the excess was wiped away with a soft cloth. When the glass was turned over, colors and tinsel showed through it clearly, and the tinseled motifs took on a softer sheen.*

neat and colorful bouquet on a cloth window shade were baffled by velvet's yielding, fuzzy texture.

Discreet advertisements began to appear in newspapers and periodicals: *Theorem Painting* for a modest fee, one could enroll in a correspondence course in theorem painting. The teacher would send formulas for preparing paints and instructions for using them on velvet, with stencils, in a prescribed and orderly manner. Female academies added theorem painting to the curriculum; private lessons were taken by mature ladies, in their homes. Once again, the old familiar fruit-basket stencils came into their own. This time, however, their effect was totally different, and surrealistic. Apples, pears and grapes hovered just above the basket container while smaller strawberries, cherries, plums, and leaves seemed to float over and around the heavier elements of the design.

Having learned the technique of applying paint to velvet, more talented ladies went on to use their stencils as they pleased, or even to paint freehand. As its name suggests, theorem painting was too regimented and mathematically exact to be very exciting.

Yet, paintings on velvet did glow with color, and seemed to be raised above their soft backgrounds. Some were given gilded frames and protective glass covering, and a place of prominence on the parlor wall. Others were used as fire screens, bellpulls, cushion tops, and coverings for boxes of all sizes.

In the final years of the eighteenth century and the first quarter of the **PAINTING** nineteenth, painting on glass was much in vogue in England and, to a lesser **ON GLASS** extent, in the United States. The art had been developed by professionals to decorate the heads of mirrors, and the showiest and most elegant decorated mirrors were those to which gold or silver leaf was applied in small stenciled motifs. The design was outlined in black paint and covered with gold size. Gold leaf was then applied, and the excess was easily wiped away. Finally, a black, gray, or white background was painted around the design. Later, paint was used on the sectional glass doors of shelf clocks, to hide the pendulum and the works; solid backgrounds with vignettes of landscapes, patriotic emblems, or portraits of Washington or Lafayette were separated by a wooden-strip divider from the clear-glass shields of the clock faces.

As a home craft, painting on glass was of a pictorial nature. Landscapes and small portraits were sometimes attempted, but the favorite subject seems to have been a still life of fruit or flowers. What distinguished this from all other forms of decorative painting was that it had to be done in reverse, on the back of the glass. A mirror image differs greatly from a head-on view, and a painting that appeared quite perfect developed unsuspected flaws when turned over and seen, through the glass, from the other side.

Taking their cue from the effective mirror heads, ladies learned to com- *Tinsel Painting* bine colors with metal foils. Gold and silver leaf were expensive, so they found a substitute in tinsel, which surprised them by looking, under glass, like clear glass. By adding sizing and thin tinfoil to old familiar stencils, they achieved glistening glass containers, glittering flowers and fruits that seemed to have been touched with frost.

In England, early in the nineteenth century, tinsel paintings were offered for sale in do-it-yourself kits. Each packet contained a hand-colored print of a famous actor costumed for a Shakespearean role, and a set of machine-stamped pieces of foil to be fitted over certain sections of the costume and accessories. Parts of the costume were to be cut away, and the remainder was to be pasted over bright-colored satin or brocade; then the precut foil accents were to be laid over their outlines on paper or cloth, and glued in place. In framing, the glass was tight-pressed against the picture so that it appeared to be a painting-on-glass.

TRANSFERS By mid-century, transfer patterns began to replace the more messy stencils for use on furniture, china, window shades, and other household objects. These were mere outlines, to be filled in with paint, and they came with printed instructions—rather like the "numbered canvas" of today.

Decals Then came decalcomania—colored transfers especially designed for use on china, glass or marble, etc.—which was followed in turn by decals that could be applied to any hard surface. All three types of transfer were made of gelatin on thin paper; when the paper was dipped in water, the design could be quickly and carefully slipped off. Considerable dexterity was involved in sliding the transfer from the paper onto the surface to be decorated—once in place, its position could not be changed.

In the final years of the nineteenth century, "cottage furniture" became very popular; it was made for use in country houses, summer homes, and children's rooms, and was quite plain and sturdy in contrast to the spindly chairs and fretwork tables of the same period. In the most expensive "bedroom suites," all the pieces of the set were painted alike, usually a pastel color. The drawers of the chifforobe, the dresser, and the dressing table were decorated with decals of flowers, fruits, pagodas, or almond-eyed maidens in kimonos and obis, carrying parasols. (Japan had opened her ports to world trade for the first time, and anything Japanese was much admired.) The same suite of furniture, unfinished, was much less expensive and could be painted and decorated with decals at home. This practice, begun by artistic but impecunious housewives, became a vaunted small economy of the wealthy.

Decals were wonderful, thought the ladies of the McKinley period—much more artistic and exact in every way than anything they could paint themselves, and there were so many interesting patterns from which to choose. Once and for all, they decided, the problems of painted decorations had been solved.

III
HAND
WEAVING
RUG MAKING
AND DYEING

In seventeenth-century America every woman, married or single, was a spinster! Flaxseed, brought by the earliest immigrants, grew well in all the colonies, and the first American-made cloth was linen. After the flax stems were beaten to a pulp, the fibers were combed and spun into thread on a small flax wheel; these were sold and repaired by the same wheelwrights who made wheels for wagons and carriages. The spun thread was measured into "knots" by a clock-reel, which was a circle of knobbed spokes with a circumference of fifty-four inches. Thread was wound around it as it turned, and at the end of its fortieth revolution the reel made a loud cracking sound—at this point, the spinster stopped the reel and tied a knot in the thread.

A few sheep were early introduced into New England, but it was many years before wool was produced in quantity. Shivering settlers lined their linen cloaks with fur, which was plentiful, but found it a poor substitute for "good English woolen." As more and more sheep were imported and bred, most homes found space for the larger spinning wheel required for wool; this was called a "walking-wheel" because the spinster paced backward and forward as she deftly twisted the fibres and fed them onto its circling rim.

From the first, most towns and villages had professional weavers who took over the task of turning homespun linen and wool thread into cloth. In the eighteenth and early nineteenth centuries, itinerant weavers hauled their looms in wagons from one farmstead to another, making up the housewife's accumulation of thread into yard-wide material before moving on. However, on solitary farms and in many scattered hamlets of New England and the Middle Colonies, cloth was a home product from flax harvest (or sheepshearing) to the finished article.

All weaving is done on a base of taut parallel threads, called a warp. The long weft thread is shuttled back and forth across the warp. In any single passage, the weft goes under alternate threads; on the return passage, it must go over those threads and under the ones it missed before.

In the colonies, little girls learned the principles of weaving on miniature lap looms. This simple device was a thin board shaped like a beaver's tail. The rounded oval paddle narrowed to a shaft with a semi-circular indentation on each side; pressed firmly between the knees, this handle held the loom steady on the weaver's lap. Across the center of the oval paddle, a row of narrow vertical slits alternated with slender slats. Each slat had a hole bored in it with a heated wire, and through these holes the warp

WEAVING

Old Looms

37

14. *In the Museum Shop of the Saconesset Homestead at West Falmouth, Massachu-*
setts, reproductions of many items in the Homestead's extensive collection are for sale.
Included are tape looms such as this lyre-shaped one of carved oak, with indentations
on each side of the handle that made it possible to grip the lap loom between the knees.
Also shown are an oven peel, pie peel, boot form and andirons.

threads were passed. The ends of the warp threads, knotted together, were held in the weaver's left hand. With the aid of a ribbon-bobbin, the weft was woven over and under threads from right to left. Then the warp ends were transferred to the right hand while the left hand plied the bobbin in the opposite direction. Beginning weavers made simple white linen tapes; by the age of six or seven, as their skill increased, they graduated to shoe laces, belts, suspenders, and hat bands, and finally to colorful "ribands."

Some tape looms, mounted in wooden boxes, were made to be rested on a table top when in use. In skilled adult hands, these tiny looms produced intricately patterned silk or woolen braid to trim clothing, bed and window valances, and cushions. The portable looms were often taken along on visits. As one colonial lady wrote to a friend in England, " 'Tis the fashion here to carry our work abroad with us, so that having company . . . is no interruption."

The wooden cloth looms of the colonial period were large—five or six feet wide, and seven to ten feet long—and the weaver sat at one end on a backless bench. Alternate rows of warp threads were lifted when a treadle was pressed. The weft-filled shuttle (carved from dogwood, which does not split) slid across the loom under these raised threads, thrown from the left hand to the right. Then, the heddle having depressed the first set of threads and lifted the other, the shuttle was tossed back from right hand to left. Such looms were too unwieldy to be kept in the family's living quarters. They were often housed in an unheated loft, or in a lean-to.

Cotton

On large southern plantations, where clothing for many slaves was produced "on the place," weaving was a year-round task that was carried on in a separate small outbuilding. Here, a special type of cloth was made. Early explorers had found a species of cotton growing wild in the West Indies, and cotton fibers had been woven, dyed, and worn by the Aztecs in Mexico and the Mayas in Peru for centuries before the first Europeans settled in the New World. Seeds of Indian and Egyptian cotton, brought to the Southern Colonies in the seventeenth century, were grown successfully, but cloth was not so easily made from cotton as from flax or wool—each small, tenacious seed had to be wrested from the boll by hand before the fibers could be carded and spun. Still, cotton with its remarkable absorbent qualities made a type of clothing that was wonderfully comfortable in hot summer weather, and in the eighteenth century cotton was grown for home consumption throughout the South. In 1793, Eli Whitney's cotton gin made it possible to remove the seeds with mechanical ease, and by this time, spinning and textile mills in England and New England were ready to convert bales of cotton into sheer silky voiles and cheap sturdy "domestic."

Linsey-woolsey

Because wool was so scarce and its warmth so desirable, a new kind of cloth called linsey-woolsey was an early American invention. Its warp was of strong linen thread, with a weft of the precious wool, and it was used for all types of clothing and for every household purpose. *Homespun* was something entirely different: a coarse, scratchy burlap woven of the tow fibers that had been combed out of flax in the process of making linen thread. Homespun was too uncomfortable to use for any clothing except work aprons, so it was allotted to window and bed curtains.

In the years immediately preceding the Revolutionary War, there was an upsurge of interest in spinning and weaving. The *Morning Chronicle and London Advertiser* for January 16, 1775, quoted a letter from the colonies that read in part:

"Homespun" in the Revolutionary Period

> The Provincial Deputies of North Carolina having resolved not to drink any more tea, nor wear any more British cloth, many ladies of this Province have determined to give a memorable proof of their patriotism, and have accordingly entered into (an) honorable and spirited association. I send it to you to shew . . . how zealously and faithfully American ladies follow the laudable example of their husbands . . .

There followed the text of a resolution adopted in Edenton, North Carolina, on October 25, 1774, and the names of fifty-one ladies who had pledged themselves to drink no tea and to wear no English-made cloth.

News of the Edenton Tea Party spread north and south, and in every colony women formed similar societies, calling themselves the Daughters of Liberty. Homespun, hand-woven, and self-sewn gowns were proudly worn as a badge of patriotism, even by ladies of fashion accustomed to ordering their entire wardrobes from modish London mantuamakers.

During the War, when clothing of all kinds was sorely needed by the ragged Continental Army, New England's ministers preached many a sermon from Exodus XXXV, 25: "And all the women that were wise hearted did spin with their hands, and brought that which they had spun . . ." The distaff side of their congregations got the message, and, in response, hundreds of all-day spinning parties were held, to which each woman came carrying her own flax wheel. At one such meeting in Northboro, Massachusetts, forty-four women spun 2,223 knots of linen and tow thread, and wove one linen sheet and two towels.

In Pennsylvania, the German settlers incorporated their beloved colors, bright red and bright blue, and traditional weaving patterns brought from their homeland, into linsey-woolsey bed covers and window curtains for their houses. Heavy white linen thread formed the warp; for the weft, a single color of wool thread was combined with white wool in complex designs of interlocking circles, squares, lines, and checks. So pleasing and so practical did the coverlets of Pennsylvania prove that similar hand-woven spreads were universally popular in the eighteenth and early nineteenth centuries. Pattern books were available to professional weavers who carried them from town to town, and housewives exchanged "drafts" of favorite designs—from Maine to Georgia the patterns were the same, but each region had its own names for them. Red and blue were the colors most used, but pink, green, yellow and snuff brown were not uncommon; textured white-on-white patterns were rare, but especially beautiful.

Pennsylvania Dutch Woven Coverlets

15. *Colonial cloth looms took up so much floor space that weaving usually was done in a loft or in a separate building. At Walnut Grove Plantation near Spartanburg, South Carolina, the weaving house doubled as the schoolroom of the neighborhood Academy; the weaver sat upon a tall schoolmaster's chair instead of on the customary backless bench. Flax, cotton, wool, and indigo, for making and coloring coverlets like those shown, all were produced on the plantation. Restored Walnut Grove, built in 1765, was opened to the public in 1967.*

Weaving in Later Days   After the Revolution, the spinning wheel, the loom and the dye pot crossed the mountains with families who took up land in the newly opened western territories. While the great nineteenth-century migration toward the Pacific was in progress, living conditions in successive frontier outposts were no less primitive than in the first seventeenth-century settlements on the eastern seacoast. Even after a network of transcontinental railroads was supplying the original colonies *and* new western states with "store-bought goods," a few self-reliant individuals in the Appalachian region clung to the old ways.

In the early twentieth century, in that mountainous area, free public schools *and* money for education were nonexistent. In eastern Kentucky, Berea College charged no tuition; its students did all the work in dormitories and kitchens, and on the farm, and in addition each student worked at least ten hours a week in one of the college industries. The sale of student-made craft items helped to pay the teachers' salaries. Girls who had learned to spin and weave at home gladly made coverlets, shawls and towels at Berea to earn the schooling they would otherwise not have had.

In 1909, Miss Martha Berry opened the doors of the Berry School at Rome, Georgia, to girls. For several years, "Miss Berry's boys" had worked for their tuition; now weaving was chosen as a means of self-help for the girls. Cotton was grown on the school farm, and a new herd of angora goats furnished wool; spinning wheels were bought, and the boys built looms, copying old ones still in use in homes far back in the hills. Then Miss Berry called in mountain women to demonstrate spinning and weaving, and the girls began to reproduce coverlets and bedspreads in traditional designs—Whig Rose, Cat-Track-and-Snail-Trail, and The Chariot Wheel.

Other schools in the Appalachian area (notably the Pi Beta Phi Settlement School at Gatlinburg, Tennessee) helped to preserve the art of weaving by teaching the craft, and fine handwoven articles are now being produced in old and new designs by members of the Southern Highland Handicraft Guild. The Guild was formed in 1930 by representatives of craft centers scattered throughout the mountains. Its purpose was to preserve the area's heritage of traditional and indigenous crafts, and to maintain high standards of quality; its members were selected for their proven ability in craftwork. Through the years, the Guild's membership has grown to include more than 500 individuals and groups in nine states: Kentucky, Tennessee, Maryland, Virginia, West Virginia, North Carolina, South Carolina, Alabama, and Georgia.

Renewed emphasis is being placed on weaving by craft centers in New England and the Middle West; for the time being, at least, this early American decorative craft has been rescued from oblivion.

PRINTED CLOTH   During the time when immigrants were flocking to the American colonies, printed materials were very popular in England and on the European continent. Block printing, invented in China, had been known in Europe since the sixth century, but printed cloth was not in general use until the British and Dutch East India Companies began to import great quantities of sprigged muslin, flowered calico, and patterned chintz in the early eighteenth century. Soon English-made cotton cloth was being printed in imitation of East Indian designs, but British ladies preferred the imported

16. *In the Museum Shop at Saconesset Homestead, an original eighteenth-century hand-woven coverlet in the traditional indigo blue and white is shown beside an exact reproduction of it made at the Handweaver's Shop of Saco, Maine. Although early coverlets followed certain established patterns, each was slightly different; every weaver indulged his own whim in setting up and treadling his loom.*

17. *In 1856, a transplanted Kentuckian, James F. Bybee, built a commodious two-story home on Sauvie Island in the Oregon Territory. On this far frontier, the furnishings of an earlier period were once again appropriate: rag rugs, spinning wheels and deal tables (above) moved west along with pioneer crafts and craftsmanship. Except for the large window with its clear glass panes, this room might have existed a hundred and fifty years before, and three thousand miles away.*

18. *In the Museum of Early Southern Decorative Arts at Winston-Salem is this Catawba bedroom (top right), from a country house built about 1811. The hand-woven rug combines the putty-green of the painted woodwork with the bright red of the block-printed linen curtains and ruffled bed skirt which show a pastoral scene and overscale flowers. Brunschwig & Fils, a New York firm noted for its collection of documentary fabrics, selected this French Provincial toile as typical of those used in the southern colonies at the time.*

19. *The cotton material (bottom right), called Williamsburg Ápples, is adapted from an eighteenth-century printed linen quilt by F. Schumacher and Company, a New York textile firm which makes fabric reproductions for Colonial Williamsburg.*

materials, which were of superior quality. In 1720, to protect the weaving industry in England, Parliament prohibited the importation of printed cottons from the Orient, and the ban continued in effect for many years; the embargo applied to the colonies as well as to the mother country.

British weavers employed printing blocks made by a method that had remained virtually unchanged for centuries and is still in use today. On a heavy block of wood with a short handle rounded to fit the palm, a design was carved in relief or intaglio. A raised pattern, with the background cut away around it, prints in color on the neutral cloth. An incised design is just the opposite. The shaped background (usually a circle, an oval, or a square) is left high while the pattern itself is cut away. Such a block prints the background in color, while the motif repeats the color of the cloth. Most English prints were single-color designs on white; for each additional color a separate block had to be used, and oversetting one color with another required patience and skill.

Whole shiploads of English printed cotton were sent to the colonies, but the price was extremely high. Ingenious Americans soon learned that they, too, could print designs on less expensive plain white imported cloth, or on locally woven linen.

Stick Printing   Cabinet makers carved wooden printing blocks for professional weavers, copying the designs of imported cloth or creating new and simpler patterns. Some of these blocks were large, as were their English models; others were extremely small, from one-half inch to an inch in diameter. In these "stick-stamps," which were especially handy for single flower motifs and for borders, Americans were borrowing a process known in Egypt for thousands of years, and they adapted it to solve the problem of printing in more than one color. Using several of the tiny blocks (each with a different flower or leaf carved in relief) and several pads impermeated with various dyes, colonial artisans created charming multicolored floral patterns.

Colonial housewives bought printing blocks from cabinet makers, or pestered husbands to try their skill at carving. Using a block and a pad of lint soaked in the ever-present indigo dye-pot, they found it relatively easy to transform a plain piece of cloth into a colorful patterned fabric. A woman who did not own, and could not borrow, a wooden printing block could make a crude substitute by cutting a small design on the smooth surface of a potato-half impaled on a stick handle. Valances and skirts for tall four-poster beds, window curtains, upholstery for chairs and sofas—all were made of hand-blocked linen to embellish eighteenth century homes.

Early American print designs were less complicated than their British and East Indian prototypes, smaller, and more widely spaced. Bright blue and bright red were the colors commonly employed, and white the favorite background for them. The effect was crisp, clean, and uncluttered. During the Federal Period, eagle and star motifs took precedence over the earlier stylized flowers, fruits, and birds.

20. *This bedspread shows the intricate tree-of-life design so popular in England and the colonies during the eighteenth century. At first, these large prints were brought from the Orient by the East India Company. When a Parliamentary embargo stopped the importation of printed cottons, Indian designs were copied by British weavers. This faithful reproduction, made by Brunschwig & Fils, is shown in the Bybee-Howell House at Sauvie Island, Oregon.*

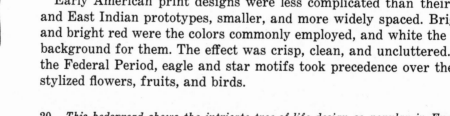

Stick printing is a craft beloved of twentieth-century camp counsellors and scout leaders. Block printing, too, has its latter-day devotees, though linoleum has well-nigh replaced wood as the surface to be carved. Instead of a dye-pad, a paint roller dipped in textile paint or in hot liquid dye is employed to ink the block, and the color is set with a hot iron (using a pressing cloth dampened with a solution of four tablespoons of white vinegar to one cup of water). In any century, the success of a block print depends upon tasteful design, skillful carving, and clear, pleasing color.

"RUGES AND CARPETS"

The "Ruges and Carpets" mentioned in early seventeenth-century inventories were not floor coverings—no housewife would have permitted so valuable and decorative a possession to be walked on! Imported at great expense from the Near East or from Flanders, they were hung on the wall in the manner of tapestries, draped across tables, or spread over beds. In the first permanent homes of New England, the floor of the keeping room (which served as kitchen, dining room, parlor, and sometimes bedroom) was strewn with sand. Each morning the patches of sand that were spotted with grease or candle wax were scooped up and thrown away; the sand was smoothed, and a decorative pattern was swirled over its surface with a turkey wing.

Soon colonial homemakers were hankering after the floor coverings that already had become popular in England and on the continent. Braided rush mats could not take the place of colorful carpets from the Orient, but they were deemed a step in the right direction. Rush mats were rapidly replaced by rag rugs, and in the Middle Colonies these continued in vogue throughout the colonial period. Strips of carpet could be woven by threading a cloth loom with a wide-spaced warp of extra-heavy linen or cotton cord. For the weft, discarded clothing, patched linens, worn-out upholstery and curtain materials were cut into inch-wide strips that were sewn together end to end. Sometimes the strips were dyed and woven in wide horizontal bands; more often the strips were left untreated and the resulting rug had narrow stripes of random colors.

BRAIDED RUGS

Not every colonial household had a loom, but any housewife could produce a rag rug with no other tool than a large needle. Worn clothing and frayed linens were cut into two-inch strips that were folded with the raw edges inside, sewed together end to end, and braided. Beginning at the center, the braid was coiled in concentric circles and stitched in place with heavy thread. Obviously, the resulting carpet was either round or oval. Occasionally, broad bands of solid colors succeeded each other from center to border, but most often the cloth strips were left undyed so braids and rug were multicolored. These were area rugs in the original sense of the word, and for many years no attempt was made to cover the entire floor with carpeting.

Braided rugs have never ceased to be popular for rooms furnished in the early American style, and machine-made copies of colonial patterns are everywhere available in department stores. Mail-order catalogues and hobby shops offer curling tips (to fold a narrow length of cloth neatly, with the cut edges inside) and directions that advocate the use of new cotton cloth braided by colors and sewn together in broad bands.

Directions for Braiding

In braiding a small oval rug in which several colors will be combined, be sure all the cloth is of approximately the same weight. Wash new cotton cloth (to remove sizing and eliminate residual shrinkage) and cut or tear the material lengthwise into two-inch strips. Join the strips by trimming their ends diagonally and sewing them together on the bias. Thread three long strips onto braiding tips, which will automatically fold the cloth into a smooth tube as they are moved along. Fasten the ends of the strips (behind the braiding tips) with safety pins to a small pillow. Plait the folded strips—left over right, and right over left—keeping the braid taut and the loops of the plait even, and pushing the folding tips ahead with the heels of the palms. As the braid is made, wind it for convenient safekeeping around the pillow.

Assemble the rug on a large table. Cut a six-inch length of braid, tuck the tip of each strip down inside its tube, and stitch across the end of the braid, sewing the three strips together. Encircle this core with ring after ring of braid. Using a bodkin-needle and carpet thread, lace the strips together by sewing through the outside strand of the braid already coiled, and then through the outside strand of the braid being added; bring the thread back across the new braid at an angle to begin the next stitch. Pause occasionally to lift the rug and drop it on the table to be sure it lies flat. Lacing too loose will allow the rows to ripple; lacing too tight will cause the rug to pucker. To add a band of different color, diagonally cut the ends of the two braids to be joined, insert the tip of each strand into its own tube, butt the two sets of strands together, and whip-stitch their edges neatly. When the desired size is reached, cut off the plait and tuck back the tip of each strand; then angle a short end of the braid under the previous row and stitch it firmly. Encircle the whole rug with a finishing strip of braid, butting its ends and sewing them together before lacing this edging to the rug. Such a rug is not only machine washable, but reversible.

HOOKED RUGS

Hooked rugs were Scandinavian in origin, but they had been used in England before the first settlement in North America. In the colonies, these were sometimes made of rag strips cut half an inch to an inch wide and rolled; however, heavy woolen yarn was found easier to work with. Burlap or loosely woven canvas was stretched (one area at a time) in a standing, slanted wooden frame, and a design was traced or drawn freehand on it. A steel-tipped wooden hook, like a gigantic crochet needle, was punched through the material from above, catching the yarn and drawing it up through the hole; when the hook was disengaged, a loop of yarn remained above the surface. Straight rows of even loops gave the carpet a smooth surface, but it was difficult for a novice to make all the loops the same length; consequently, the tops of the loops frequently were sheared off in a chenille effect. As a change from invariably circular braided carpets, hooked rugs were usually square or oblong.

At first the range of color was necessarily limited, and the designs were geometric: blocks, or combinations of squares and circles. Then stylized flowers were enclosed in the circles, and colors became brighter. By the mid-eighteenth century, complex colorful scrolls, leaves and blossoms were arranged in garlands or medallions—such patterns were inspired, perhaps, by imported Aubusson carpets.

In the first half of the nineteenth century, many hooked rugs depicted full-rigged ships breasting white-capped waves. Animal and bird motifs were popular, too: the stag at bay, the St. Bernard with his keg of brandy, the American eagle in full flight. Predictably, the late Victorian era was a time for mottoes and Bible texts, worked in black on a white ground, with wide black borders almost hidden by full-blown roses and white lilies.

Most of the machine-made room-size hooked rugs now sold in department stores are in eighteenth-century Aubusson-type floral designs. Smaller accent rugs that imitate seventeenth-century block patterns are also factory produced, and hearth rugs bearing early nineteenth-century eagle or sailing-ship motifs are pictured in mail-order catalogs.

Rug hooking has probably been the most continually popular of all colonial crafts, and in the twentieth century it still provides ample scope for artistic ability and good workmanship. Many talented hooked-rug makers prefer to work in the traditional manner, from the top of the design, with a hand-hook. This type of hooking can be done without a frame, on the lap, and allows great flexibility of design and delicacy of color shading. It goes slowly; an experienced worker can do one square foot of hooking in about six hours. Rug makers who create their own original designs often use strips of woolen cloth and obtain unusual color patterns by dyeing the cloth themselves. However, most beginners (and a great many experts) avail themselves of rug yarns in cotton or mothproofed wool that come in a wide range of light and dark shades. There are mechanical hooks available (sold in needlework shops with complete directions for their use) that greatly speed up the hooking process. With these, the rug is hooked from the back, and a frame must be used to keep the canvas taut. Of course, the stamped side of the canvas still faces the worker, but the wool is punched through the backing from above instead of being drawn up from below. The length of the loops is automatically and evenly controlled.

Directions for Hooking

The easiest possible way to make a large hooked rug is in one- or two-foot squares which are sewed together after hooking. One great advantage of this method is that the work is light and portable, but a hand hook must be used.

Buy ready-stamped squares of rug canvas, or trace your own designs on cut burlap. If you buy stamped canvas, the edges will already be bound. If you cut your own burlap squares, their edges should be machine stitched to prevent ravelling before the design is traced and hooking begins. Be sure to leave a one-inch border of unhooked canvas around each square, for sewing the pieces together. Rug yarn is sold in large hanks and should be cut in advance for easier use; twenty-four inches is considered a convenient length.

With the left hand, press a strip of yarn lightly against the back of the canvas. With the right hand, insert the steel tip of the hook through a hole in the top of the canvas, catch the yarn, and draw a loop back through the hole; make the loop about one-third inch high, and disengage the hook. Skip three threads, push the hook through again, and draw up a second loop, making it the same height as the first. Always outline each motif with hooking; fill in that motif completely before going on to another.

Hook the background last. When all the squares are finished, turn back their edges, leaving a three-thread selvage around the square; baste the turned edges to the back of the canvas. Fit two squares together, selvage over selvage, and sew them together with carpet thread and a curved rug-needle. The final rows of hooking on the two squares should just touch. Add squares, making a vertical strip. Finally, sew strips together to complete the rug. Twenty one-foot squares will make a hearth rug five feet long and four feet wide. Later, the size can be increased by adding other strips; if a square is stained or burned, it can be removed and a new piece inserted.

In their natural state, wool and linen fibers are drab. Wool has a dirty grayish cast, and linen is yellowish tan; linsey-woolsey combines the worst color features of both. With hard work and ingenuity, colonial housewives were able to change these sturdy but unprepossessing materials into reasonable facsimiles of the cloth they had known at home. Linen, washed in buttermilk and spread out to dry in the hot summer sun, bleached to ecru; a second and a third bleaching were required to turn it snowy white. Wool was washed many times in warm water with goose grease or bear fat added to smooth the fibers, and then was steeped in dye. The finest wool thread, intended for a best dress or a Sunday coat, was dyed before being woven. Cloth made from dyed thread kept its true color so well that "dyed in the wool" became a synonym for constancy and devotion to purpose. **DYEING**

In every household, a clay dye pot was always at the ready; usually it contained a deep rich indigo blue. From the earliest days, itinerant peddlers made their way on foot to the most isolated outposts, and their packs contained needles, pins, and lumps of indigo. At first, indigo was imported from the Far East and the West Indies. Early in the 1740's, Eliza Lucas (Pinckney) was left behind in South Carolina *at the age of sixteen* to manage three large mainland plantations when her father assumed his duties as Governor of Antigua. With plants sent back from the islands, she began a series of experiments; indigo adapted so well to the marshy South Carolina lowlands that it soon became an important crop in that colony and in Louisiana. From this basic dye (depending upon dilution) came every shade from palest ice to deepest midnight blue, and its availability explains the prevalence of blue and white as a color scheme in early American textiles. *Indigo*

Any color, of course, was better than no color at all, but everlasting blue grew tiresome. Colonial women began to test plant dyes made from the bark of trees and the juices of wild berries. They discovered a native variety of the madder plant, from which all shades of red had been derived in Europe, and madder red rivaled indigo blue in popularity. *Plant Dyes*

They also found that dogwood bark yielded a clear and beautiful red dye. Pokeberry juice colored cloth a rich crimson; the juice of sumac berries turned it gray. Browns and tans were obtained from walnut and butternut hulls; linsey-woolsey took butternut dye especially well. Yellowroot acquired its name from its valuable dye properties, but yellow and orange could also be derived from birchbark and sassafras roots. Black oak bark, plus alum, provided an acceptable though rather greenish black; fresh walnut roots produced black with a brownish cast; the leaves and fruit of the gallberry bush gave a true black that was used by hatters and professional weavers. Out of the vegetable patch came magenta (from beets) and saffron yellow (from onion skins.) Grape juice lent a tinge of purple to white linen, and the juice of wild cherries colored it rosy red. The light yellow-green of boiled grass was a particularly permanent dye, as anyone who has ever tried to remove an accidental grass stain knows. A deep blue-green resulted when the juice of goldenrod blossoms was mixed with indigo and alum. Violet-colored juice from the petals of wild or garden iris tinted the wool from white sheep to a delicate lavender, and deep purple could be brewed from cedar tops.

Redyeing   Newly made thread, woven linens and woolens were not the only materials that found their way into the dye pot. Cloth of any kind was valuable; when it was worn beyond use, it was first redyed a darker color, then raveled into its component threads, and rewoven. This practice was common in affluent households as well as in the homes of farmers and artisans.

Although attempts were made in several colonies to establish a silk industry, all were ultimately unsuccessful. Fragile imported silk was so expensive that it could never in conscience be discarded, but it soon wore threadbare. When raveled silk was rewoven, it often was combined with sturdier linen or wool threads to increase its durability. Martha Washington, for example, made it a rule to dye her old silk gowns to a desired color, ravel them carefully onto bobbins, and have them rewoven with linen or cotton for chair seats and cushion covers; and the process was sometimes repeated in reverse. She was particularly fond of a certain red and white gown, and enjoyed explaining to visitors that its white stripes were of Mount Vernon's own cotton while the red were of silk from worn-out chair covers and the General's discarded stockings!

IV HISTORIC NEEDLE CRAFT

Quilting, an art that had been practised for centuries in China before it came into use in Europe, reached the height of its popularity in England and the Low Countries during the seventeenth century. Quilted satins, silks, and velvets were fashionable for cloaks and doublets; warm quilted bed-coverings were made of handwoven linen or of India chintz. Whether the end product was intended to dress a person or a bed, the method was the same: a thin layer of wool or goosedown was sandwiched between two lengths of cloth; the edges were sewn together and the mat was stretched flat in a wooden frame. Patterned stitching then joined the top and bottom materials together and held the lining in place, and this quilting step gave its name to the finished work. The simplest quilting covered the surface of the mat with close-spaced parallel rows of tiny running stitches or with a criss-cross pattern of vertical and horizontal lines, but often the quilting was so intricate in design that it became a test of skill and a demonstration of artistry. This practical art, brought to the colonies by the earliest English and Dutch settlers, developed over the years into something peculiarly American.

The pieced "Crazy Quilt" is an American innovation that evolved gradually from an accidental beginning. Warm bed quilts were an absolute necessity in colonial households, and originally their surfaces, top and bottom, were of linen. When one of these developed a worn spot, it was carefully patched with whatever material came to hand; as time passed, the basic linen covering might disappear entirely beneath overlapping patches. The colonists, constantly in search of color and ornamentation for their homes, found the patched quilts more attractive than plain new ones.

Crazy Quilts

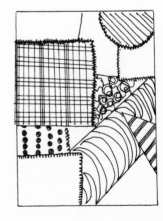

Women to whom a length of cloth meant hundreds of hours spent in carding, spinning, weaving and dyeing, were naturally chary of it. But no matter how carefully they placed their patterns in cutting out clothing, small irregularly shaped pieces of material were left over. As an exercise in economy, housewives began to piece together these bits of cloth too small for any other use; from fifty to a hundred scraps were needed to form a surface large enough to cover a bed. These crazy quilts had no pattern or predominant color. *Any* available scraps of cloth were used, and the pieces were fitted together like a jig-saw puzzle.

Next in the development of American quilts came the "hit-or-miss." Pieces of cloth were cut in squares of uniform size to make them easier to sew together, but they were placed without regard for color or for the

Pieced Quilts

texture of the material. Then colors were sorted, arranged in rows to form a Roman stripe, or joined in alternating light and dark squares in a checkerboard effect. Finally, triangular and diamond shaped quilt pieces came into use. With these, circular designs could be made, and all-over patterns became popular.

Perhaps the most universally used piecework pattern was the block design made of diamond shapes of different widths. By carefully combining light, medium and dark colors, a three-dimensional trompe l'oeil effect was produced: row after row of cubes balanced on edge, like a child's building blocks.

Quilt piecing was considered child's work. The precious bits of linen, calico, chintz, and linsey-woolsey (shaped and "laid out" by adult hands) were stitched together by little girls just learning to sew.

These pieced coverlets were often tasteful and sometimes extremely artistic, but the real aristocrats of the craft were the appliquéd, or patchwork, quilts. On a large piece of white cloth, small bright-colored patches —squares, diamonds, circles, triangles—were arranged in a pattern and basted in place; then their edges were couched or embroidered, often in thread of a contrasting hue. Usually the component patches of a design were pieced together before the whole pattern was applied to the cloth. Patchwork quilts required more time and skill than piecework, but were infinitely more pleasing to the eye.

Patchwork Quilts

Flowers, sunbursts, stars, and shells grew to be favorite motifs, and often the design of the appliquéd patches was repeated in intricate background quilting. Some traditional patterns bore historic names, such as Charter Oak, Eagle and Star, Log Cabin, or Confederate Rose; others (among them Garden of Eden, Joseph's Coat, and Cross-and-Crown) had Biblical connotations. Sometimes the pattern names were descriptive of the motifs, as Rising Sun, Pine Tree, or Flower Basket; sometimes the names were fanciful and charming, as Delectable Mountains, or Grandmother's Flower Garden. As a general rule, a design was known by the same name throughout the colonies.

Once the quilt top was pieced and/or patched, it was given a backing of plain, sturdy material and a thin smooth lining for warmth. At first, wool was used exclusively for filling, but when cotton began to be grown extensively, it was welcomed as a substitute; cotton batting was cheaper, and easier to sew. In very early quilts, no effort was made to remove the cotton seeds.

A quilting frame consisted of four long padded bars of wood, crossed and tied firmly at the corners to form a rectangle. The layered material, basted together around the edges, was pulled taut and sewed to the frame with heavy thread. Then the frame was raised on chairs or saw-horses to a

Quilting Frame

21. *The house in which young Lt. U. S. Grant lived while stationed in Detroit in 1849 is now located on the Michigan State Fairgrounds. Under the auspices of the Detroit Historical Museum, it has been furnished with authentic pieces from the period when Ulysses S. Grant was President of the United States, 1868-1876. The collection includes the delightful Victorian silk crazy quilt, (opposite) bordered with velvet. Embroidered flower sprays or pictures brighten squares of unpatterned silk; there is a political badge, a lady in a poke bonnet, and even a needlework cartoon—a wind-swept, hatless gentleman with his umbrella turned inside out.*

convenient height. When about a foot on each side was fully quilted, the frame was untied, the finished edges were rolled up on the bars, and the corners lashed together again; the visible surface of the quilt grew smaller and smaller as the work progressed. One person, moving her chair along each bar as she worked, could do all the quilting herself, and women in solitary homes often did so. However, as many as a dozen quilters could sit facing each other around the frame, stitching the three layers together in an agreed-upon decorative design.

Most seventeenth- and eighteenth-century quilts were very nearly square —not long enough by present-day standards, but quite right for the shorter bedsteads of the period. Our ancestors were not all stunted in height. They slept in a half-reclining position, well propped up on bolsters and pillows!

An especially handsome quilt was a treasured possession to be kept for "company best" and to be handed down as an heirloom. In her will dated May 20, 1778, Mary Ball Washington bequeathed to her son George her "best bed, bedstead, and . . . quilted blue-and-white quilt."

Friendship Quilts

Throughout the nineteenth century in the Middle West, where farms were large and towns widely scattered, the farmer's wife led a lonely life. A quilting bee brought neighbors from miles around together for much needed companionship; like the spinning parties in New England during the Revolutionary War, this was an all-day affair. Recipes and gossip were exchanged as the quilters vied with each other in taking small, even, rapid stitches. A bountiful midday "spread" broke the tedium; before the guests left for home, a new quilt was completed and its edges neatly hemmed. A specialty of midwestern quilting bees was the Friendship Quilt. On colored patches, the friends who attended the party and helped with the sewing signed their names in ink, and the autographs were later embroidered by the hostess in white thread.

More often seen in the east was another type of Friendship Quilt in which each square was designed and appliquéd by a different person. The sections were put together with colored or embroidered bands of material to form the top of the quilt. Each square was signed (in ink or in embroidery) with the name or monogram of the donor. Such quilts were made for brides, or as presentation pieces for persons of prominence.

22. *In 1849, the Baroness Pontalba began the building of America's first apartment house alongside Jackson Square in New Orleans. The building still is occupied; one section of it has been restored by the Louisiana State Museum as the Pontalba 1850 House, and decorated as it might have been when the block was new. On a massive four-poster bed (opposite) a block-patterned quilt is displayed. Its surface is composed of plain and patterned silk triangles; light and dark colors are so combined that the design appears to be raised. The quilt, made about 1850, is finished with silk fringe that repeats the colors of the blocks.*

Crazy Quilt Revived   Late in the nineteenth century the pieced Crazy Quilt enjoyed a revival. These Victorian silk quilts were sentimental as a lacy Valentine. Pieces from satin wedding gowns, "Little Lord Fauntleroy" velvet suits, little-girl taffeta party dresses, and striped silk cravats made the finished "throw" a cherished family record as personal as a diary. They were display pieces, made to be draped over the parlor table, swagged across one corner of a square piano, or folded at the foot of a day bed.

Quilting Today   Although quilts are no longer a household necessity, in many parts of the country quilting remains a favorite form of needlework. Small, easy-to-handle crib quilts and long, rectangular quilted bedspreads are available in kit form at department stores and hobby shops; but experienced quilters prefer the challenge of more difficult traditional designs. Singly, or in groups that meet at community clubs and senior citizens' centers, they recreate such familiar and beloved quilt patterns as Double Wedding Ring and World Without End.

23. *The Bedford Museum, in Bedford, New York, lists among its many treasures the appliquéd friendship quilt (below) presented to Mr. Heroy, the pastor of the Bedford Presbyterian Church from 1857 to 1879. The multiwindowed, steepled building is a faithful representation of the church as it then looked. Each of the eighty-one squares is signed in ink by a young parishioner.*

24. *The Nathaniel Russell House, built in Charleston, South Carolina, before 1809, and now the property of the Historic Charleston Foundation, is one of America's outstanding examples of Adam architecture. On a graceful tester bed (opposite) is an unusually beautiful friendship quilt containing thirty-six squares, each with a different appliquéd floral-chintz design. The quilt is believed to have been made about 1800, for a bride; each square is signed with the name or monogram of the friend whose work it was.*

Stumpwork   In the eighteenth century, quilting methods were used to produce a type of needlecraft called *stumpwork,* or *trapunto.* A painted or embroidered picture on a square of silk or linen was outline-quilted to a backing of coarser material; as the quilting was done, portions of the design were padded—some heavily, others very lightly—to obtain a three-dimensional effect. Examples of old stumpwork are rather rare, but the craft has recently been rediscovered by creative needlewomen who apply this technique to hand-blocked linen or silk prints.

Since the eighteenth century, raised quilting has been used on clothing and bedspreads, to create not pictures but motifs. When trapunto first became popular, an entire petticoat or coverlet often was covered with close-spaced raised designs; at this time, the favorite padding was soft milkweed down.

25. *White Sulphur Springs was a famous spa when West Virginia became a state during the Civil War. In the mid-1800's, a handsome private cottage on the resort's grounds became known as the President's Cottage because so many Chiefs of State— Tyler, Van Buren, Fillmore, Pierce, and Buchanan—made it their Summer White House. This bedroom is dominated by a fine quilted patchwork spread, with huge bright-red oak leaves appliquéd on a white background. A woven rag rug, of plaid design, lies beside the turned bed of maple and pine. At the foot of the bed is an oak cradle from the colonial period, painted a typical dark green.*

A sampler, as the name implies, was first intended to be a reference SAMPLERS work; on a single piece of cloth, an accomplished needlewoman would preserve her complete repertoire of embroidery patterns, drawnwork, lettering, and fancy stitches. In seventeenth century England, samplers were long and narrow—about eight inches wide and a yard or more in length. Fragments of designs and examples of stitches were scattered over the entire surface. As it was worked, the sampler was rolled up, scroll fashion. It could be tucked away in a chest or a drawer until needed, and unrolled to permit the seamstress to select the proper motif for decorating clothing, chair covers, bed hangings, and cushions.

26. *This sampler, cross-stitched in silk on linen, hangs at Woodlawn Plantation in Mount Vernon, Virginia. Across the top, the alphabet is worked in capitals; on the second line are Arabic numerals from one to ten and a second alphabet, in small letters. In the center, religious symbols take the place of the customary text. At the bottom, the French inscription identifies the sampler as "Made by Antoinette Le Haribel, age twelve, in the year 1820."*

In the colonies, where small girls received their first (and usually their only) schooling at home, the sampler became a teaching aid with a dual purpose. Having already mastered knitting—by the age of four a little girl was expected to be able to make plain stockings and mittens on long wooden needles—it was vitally important that a child of five should learn to sew. If she could be taught to read at the same time, so much the better. Across the top of a large square of linen, colonial mothers drew the alphabet in capital and small letters, and, underneath it, numbers from one to ten. "Great A, little a, Bouncing B . . ." As the time-honored rhyme was repeated, small fingers worked the letters in Cross or Chain Stitch, using a large needle and dark worsted thread. Literally, girls learned to sew before they learned to read, but they were not likely to forget either lesson.

As the next step, a "text" was printed in the center of the sampler, and worked with smaller needle and finer thread. This text was a quotation from the Bible, a moral sentiment, or such an applicable verse as:

> Ye springing Fair, whom gentle Minds incline
> To All that's Curious, Innocent, and Fine,
> Now let the Fingers, whose unrivalled Skill
> Exalts the Needle, grace the noble Quill.

Below the text there usually was room for an embroidered needle-picture; landscapes, houses, and Noah's Ark were favored subjects. Vines, leaves, flowers and birds (often worked in silk thread) provided a colorful border as embroidery motifs were practised. Finally, at the bottom of the composition, the name of its maker and the date of its completion were added—the little girl was often in her teens by this time, the sampler having been her constant companion for several years. The finished product was then framed and hung in a place of prominence on the wall, for a sampler was a sort of diploma as well as a piece of decorative needlework.

EMBROIDERED PICTURES

In the early eighteenth century, the stitches that had been practised on a sampler were used by ladies in embroidered maps while the leaf, flower, bird and fruit motifs reappeared exquisitely worked in silk on narrow panels of satin. These pieces of fine adult workmanship were made for wall decoration; they were framed and, usually, glazed.

A unique type of needle-picture, the coat of arms, was called a hatchment. The design was meticulously traced on linen. The embroidery threads were color-matched and the stitches were slanted to conform to the heraldic description. Since few colonial families could boast armorial bearings, a hatchment was made with loving care and displayed with pride. When a death occurred in the household, the hatchment (draped in black crepe as a symbol of mourning) was hung on the front door until the home funeral service was over, and then was transferred to the side of the hearse for the slow trip to the cemetery. Hatchments were distinguishable from ordinary coats of arms by their diamond shape, which was emphasized by narrow black frames.

By 1750, the embroidery done for wall decoration had taken the form of needlework pictures. Almost any subject a contemporary artist might portray on canvas was attempted: landscapes with buildings and ruins added; pastoral scenes complete with flower-garlanded shepherdesses and

27. *This enchanting eighteenth-century embroidered picture, from the outstanding needlework collection of the Philadelphia Museum of Art, makes up in exuberance what it lacks in perspective. The well-dressed lady and gentleman, having just emerged from their reassuringly solid house, seem amazed to find themselves in the midst of a landscape where squirrels grow as large as horses and passenger pigeons overshadow trees.*

28. *Early in the nineteenth century, romanticism became vitally important in needle-work as well as in literature. This view of Exeter, England, worked in chenille on hand-painted silk, was embroidered in 1810 by Rebecca Rooker of Baltimore, where the Misses Rooker established an English Seminary for young ladies that flourished from 1812 to 1838. The needle-picture is in the collection of the DAR Museum, in Washington, D.C.*

sheep; even portraits. White bolting cloth (a very thin silk) was the preferred background material, though satin and linen were also used; with silk floss or twisted silk thread, various stitches were combined in careful shadings of color. For contrast, the faces and hands of human figures often were painted on the cloth, and landscapes were sometimes an embroidered foreground against a painted backdrop of hills and sky. In framing, these pictures were customarily surrounded by a broad margin of black glass with a narrow gold edge.

The death of George Washington, in 1799, had an instantaneous and long-lasting effect on American embroidered pictures. Mourning scenes, showing ladies in high-waisted Empire gowns weeping before a monument shaded by a weeping willow tree, became the rage. Merchants who sold embroidery materials offered silk squares with traced patterns all ready to be filled in with shaded stitches. These funerary designs, which had never entirely disappeared, were produced in great numbers during and after the War Between the States. In keeping with the taste of the period, the willows were weepier, the female figures were garbed in black and wore flowing mourning veils, and the rest of the composition was executed in shades of sombre gray. *Mourning Pictures*

Early in the eighteenth century, advertisements in the New York and Boston newspapers featured "curtains ready stamped for working," and "crewel yarns in many diverse colours." Crewel work was not new. For centuries, European women had used slackly twisted, two-ply worsted thread to embroider linen, twill, or fustian bed hangings and chair covers. In England, such designs were especially intricate; colorful highly stylized flowers, fruits, and birds almost hid the background material. In the Low Countries, where Europe's finest weavers had produced magnificent tapestries, crewel embroidery sometimes adopted scenes from woven wall-hangings; other designs were borrowed from paintings and stressed floral garlands, bowknots, and streamers. **CREWEL WORK**

Colonial women, whose childhood samplers had been bordered with traditional embroidery motifs, found in crewel work an ideal means of adding color and ornamentation to their homes. American crewel embroidery, like many another transplanted craft, was a simplified version of its English and continental predecessors. Fewer colors and fewer types of stitches were used; the design was much more open, and the motifs less stylized.

In addition to the prestamped materials sold in city shops, patterns were available; these were passed along from one household to another, but few women followed them exactly. Some crewel designs (notably fruit-basket motifs) are identical with contemporary painted decorations on chair backs, chests, and trays, so it is logical to assume that the same set of stencils may sometimes have been used to ornament furniture and to outline embroidery. In order to obtain exactly the colors desired, many crewel-work enthusiasts preferred to dye their own yarns; talented ladies often drew their own designs, freehand.

Leaves, stems, vines, and tendrils were very important components of American designs, and the Tree of Life a favorite motif. Fruits, especially grapes, were popular, and birds were often used. Flowers, however, were considered essential, and a recognizable daisy, tulip, carnation, or thistle was a part of almost every composition.

Often an entire design was worked in a single stitch. The favorite, a variant of the Roumanian Stitch, was called New England Laid Stitch. Others commonly used were outline, buttonhole, running, flat, feather, chain, and satin. French, bullion, and coral knots contributed to the finishing touches in flower centers and birds' eyes.

Since indigo was so popular and prevalent a dye, it is hardly surprising that most surviving examples of early American crewel patterns are worked in shades of blue. Whether the yarns were monochromatic or rainbow-hued, the effect of this wide-spaced embroidery in realistic motifs was light and graceful. In some households, the principal bedchamber was given matching window and bed hangings of crewel work, in imitation of the fashionable European sets of printed cloth. More often, crewel-embroidered fabric upholstered fireside chairs or covered small cushions. Rarely, an exceptionally intricate and well-executed small design was framed as a wall hanging.

A revival of interest in this quick and not-too-difficult embroidery has inspired several excellent books that contain patterns and detailed instructions. In department stores, as well as in needlework and hobby shops, there are kits containing a stamped cloth, colored yarns, needles, and directions. These packets are for chair seats, cushion covers, wall pictures — even for ashtray backs, which by no stretch of the imagination could be considered period pieces.

FLAMESTITCH EMBROIDERY

A second very popular type of embroidery in the seventeenth and eighteenth centuries was Flamestitch, which is also called barjello, point d'Hongrie and florentine stitch. "Flamestitch," however, is a far more descriptive title for the work done in the American colonies, where red, yellow, and greenish-blue were combined and shaded to resemble tongues of fire. The thread-count stitches, staggered in length from one-fourth inch to a full inch or more, were done in silk on canvas or linen, and the colors were worked horizontally. Each repeated section of the pattern forms a tented arch, and the feeling of this embroidery is definitely Gothic.

Flamestitch borders often finished bed and window valances. An over-all flamestitch pattern was sometimes used (and occasionally was worked in wool for this purpose) to upholster a high-backed chair or a stool. More often, an over-all patterned piece was draped over a table. Flamestitch cushions were valued as brilliant color accents. Directions for this stitch are included in many manuals of embroidery, but it is rarely seen in fire-color form outside house museums. Its chief appeal lay in the rapidity with which the inch-long stitches covered cloth with cheerful hues that were especially pleasing against brown wood-paneled walls.

BERLIN WORK

By the seventeenth century, petit point embroidery had become a fine art in France and in the Low Countries. For the graceful baroque furniture of the Palace of Versailles, petit-point upholstery copied in miniature the scenic designs of earlier woven tapestries, and "tapestry work" was the misleading name given to the embroidery in England. Close-meshed canvas or linen, stretched in a stationary slanted wooden frame, was worked in finest wool, and each tiny stitch covered one thread of the cloth background.

29. *These hand-woven linen window hangings, with their delicate tracery of vines and flowers, and accents of plume-shaped leaves, are typical of the airy, wide-spaced designs of early American crewel embroidery. They are displayed in the Delaware State Room of Memorial Continental Hall in Washington, D.C.*

30. *In the heart of the city that bears his name stands William Trent's brick mansion, built in 1719 and now the property of the City of Trenton, New Jersey. After restoration, it was furnished with pieces from the William and Mary and Queen Anne periods, to approximate those of an inventory made in 1726. This black-painted stool, made about 1690, has its original covering of Flamestitch, worked in wool. The horizontally-worked, unequal stitches give the pattern the look of fire, and the colors enhance this effect.*

31. *In a bedroom at Sunnyside, once owned by Washington Irving and now maintained as part of the Sleepy Hollow Restorations of Tarrytown, New York, is a piece of Berlin Work (above right), begun about 1840. It remains unfinished; the scrim is sewn to a wooden embroidery frame. The pattern, stamped and shaded in color, is plainly visible for only a few motifs have been filled in with chenille.*

Needlepoint, or Berlin Work, done on canvas with worsted wools, was always more popular in the American colonies. Each slanted stitch covered two vertical and two horizontal threads, so the work went much faster. Scenic designs were favored for framing in firescreens; small floral patterns were used in shield-shaped or oval candle-screens and for the tops of cushions.

During the Victorian era, Berlin Work reached new heights of popularity in the United States. For the upholstery of chairs, loveseats, ottomans and footstools, innumerable clusters of red and pink roses were

32. *Berlin Work was tremendously popular in the Victorian era, and was used in a number of decorative ways. In an exhibit (right) titled "Art in the Parlor," presented by the Detroit Historical Museum, items of everyday use in the late-nineteenth century were grouped. A towel rod of East-lake style, with a panel insert of needlepoint; a framed picture, featuring the ubiquitous Victorian full-blown rose; a slipper-box stool—its padded top, upholstered in needlepoint, concealed a compartment that held a lady's shoes; a parlor cuspidor that doubled as a footstool—the hinged lid, covered with a needlepoint floral design with circular border of petit point, was raised with the foot lever visible on the right side; a lyre-shaped lady's boot jack, with a swinging panel ornamented with a design that combined needlepoint and petit point; a long bellpull, with brass mounts, is of the kind seen in well-appointed Victorian parlors and used to summon servants—against a dark needlepoint background, the scrolled design of roses and leaves is worked in bright beads.*

worked on black backgrounds. Oval needlepoint pictures (bouquets of roses, forget-me-nots, and fuchsias caught up with blue-ribbon bowknots and streamers) were given heavy gilded frames. Long, narrow bell-pulls combined centered petit-point floral panels with needlepoint backgrounds. Square piano stools and oblong piano benches repeated the roses on other furniture and added white lilies or lilies of the valley for contrast.

Needlepoint embroidery has one obvious advantage over other types of needlework: it lasts. Mid-Victorian examples, in perfect condition after a hundred years, have served as models for mid-twentieth-century commercial designs. Prestamped canvas (sometimes with petit-point centers done in Belgium) are available in department stores and needlework shops. Chair-cover kits include color-stamped canvas and matching wool. Purse kits offer (in addition to canvas and wool) directions for working monograms. And twentieth-century needlepoint wool comes mothproofed!

BEADWORK
Knitting

Knitting was not a pastime in colonial days, but a necessity; every girl (and many a boy) learned on long wooden needles at a very early age. For the exquisite patterned knitting that was a favorite type of handwork, adults used slender double-pointed needles made of ivory or bone.

As if counting stitches for lacy patterns were not hard enough, the ladies proved their skill by knitting beaded silk belts and reticules. All the beads for a row of knitting had to be threaded on the measured silk in advance, and it was no mean feat to pull one bead forward and hold it in position while a stitch was slipped from one needle to the other. Allover designs of a single color were considered elementary. Multicolored designs of flowers and birds—even lettering—were commonplace. The pattern was drawn on paper, in color, in a series of circles, with each dot representing a bead. The various colors of beads for one row of knitting were selected, and threaded on the silk in the proper order.

Bead Embroidery

In the nineteenth century, a type of beaded Berlin Work was very popular for wall pictures, bell-pulls, or firescreens. White or black worsted thread was used, with crystal or varicolored beads. The loose beads, in a flat saucer, were placed on a tabouret near the embroidery frame. A single bead was picked up with the needle, pulled down the thread to the surface of the canvas, and held steady while the stitch was completed. Bright beaded flower wreaths sparkled against a background of black needlepoint; a helmeted Minerva, in crystal beads, gleamed on a shaded gray ground.

NEEDLEWORK

When Thomas Jefferson's daughter Martha was at school near Paris in her early teens, her father wrote her this advice:

> Do not neglect your needlework. In the country life of America there will be many moments when a woman can have recourse to nothing but her needle for employment. In dull company and in dull weather, it is ill manners to read; it is ill manners to leave them; no card playing there among genteel people.

V DESIGNS WITH FRESH FLOWERS AND FRUIT

Since the beginning of recorded history, fresh flowers have gladdened the hearts and decorated the homes of civilized men. Each succeeding culture borrowed from the past, and added its own contributions of preferred plant materials, containers, and elements of design.

Greek Wreaths and Garlands

The inventive Greeks, to whom the laurel wreath was the symbol of victory, made wreaths of flowers and sweet-smelling herbs for indoor decoration. Fruit blossoms, poppies, iris, and narcissi were used, but one flower was esteemed above all others, and the Greeks had a word for it: stephanotis. Stephanos meant wreath, and stephanotis translates "fit for a crown." In winter, wreaths were made of acorns, nuts, berries, ivy, and evergreen foliage. The classic Grecian urn was introduced, but was not filled with flowers, for the Greeks did not place cut flowers in vases. Garlands of leaves, with flowers intertwined, were laid flat on tables. Fruit was allowed to spill from cornucopias or was heaped in flat baskets; the pomegranate was almost always included in an arrangement of fruit, as was the fig. Bunches of grapes, attached to a section of leafy vine, topped the composition.

Roman Swags and Sheaves

For their homes, the Romans preferred the garland to the wreath, and the hanging swag to the table garniture. Their swags were long, narrow scarves, filled with the same blossoms the Greeks had liked plus jasmine, quince blooms, and *Rosa gallica*. Sometimes flowers were loosely heaped in baskets. The Romans' own contribution to decoration was the sheaf of golden wheat, tied with ribbon, which was their symbol of fertility.

Byzantine Formality and Symmetry

During the Byzantine Period (325-600 A.D.) entirely new decorative concepts from the Near East arrived in Europe to be mingled with Greco-Roman ideas. Byzantine floral arrangements, stylized to the point of artificiality, were noted for height and symmetry. The most typical form was the tapering pyramid of foliage, dotted at regular intervals with flowers or fruit; sometimes the cone of green leaves was wound with a spiral of narrow ribbon. These tree shapes were placed in baskets or in ornamental bronze containers. For symmetry, cornucopias were used in pairs; they were hung on the wall, and filled with apples, cherries, peaches, pears, and grapes. On flat trays, flower heads and foliage were arranged in patterns that suggested a Persian carpet; lilies and roses were featured, with ferns and palm fronds.

When the wreaths and swags of ancient Greece and Rome returned to popularity during the Classic Revival Period, they were accompanied and influenced by the Byzantine concepts of stylized shape and insistent symmetry.

Gothic Realism and Symbolism   During the Gothic Period (1200-1425) learning was centered in the Church, and church sculpture was acclaimed the highest form of art. Stone leaves, fruits and flowers—in wreaths, garlands, and baskets—were realistic to the last detail, and their symbolism was of the utmost importance. Very few persons other than the clergy could read, but even the illiterate understood that the apple represented Evil. Three of anything exemplified the Trinity, so trilobed leaves and tripetalous flowers were especially valued, in churches and in homes. *Rosaries* were fresh flower wreaths; ten pink roses for Ave Marias; five red roses for Paternosters and Glorias. The Virgin Mary had her special flowers, considered appropriate for massing at the base of statues or incorporating in paintings: roses, lilies, columbines, pinks, and marigolds.

Pseudo-Gothic architecture characterized the Victorian era, and with it came a demand for realism in Art. Symbolism, too, was present, but was no longer of a religious nature; the "language of flowers" was an expression of sentimentality rather than of piety.

Twentieth-century rosaries are made of beads instead of blossoms, but the stone church carvings of the Middle Ages still influence altar arrangements. Certain flowers (notably the lily) are valued for their Biblical connotations, and the special plants associated with saints and martyrs are considered particularly appropriate for use in the sanctuary.

Renaissance Emphasis on Arrangement and Containers   In Italy, during the Renaissance (1400-1600), great artists were called upon by their princely sponsors to design lavish floral displays for pageants and festivals; garlands of fruits, flowers, and foliage festooned the walls and ceilings of new and spacious palazzi. These ephemeral decorations, copied by sculptors, were preserved to influence flower arrangers for all time to come. Luca della Robbia gave his nàme to the beautiful terra cotta wreath form in which small fruits were superimposed on a background of foliage. Andrea Mantegna carved lovely stone garlands, alternating leaves and flowers in bold groupings; in the center of each swag, he liked to mass fruits and pine cones.

Along with a heightened awareness of beauty came a reawakened interest in flower arranging for the home. Cut flowers were used in fireplaces and window embrasures, on writing tables, low benches, shelves, and even on the floor. Six-foot-tall stands, like braziers on elongated candlesticks, were placed in corners or in front of windows; in them, tall flowers were massed and long sprays of foliage were allowed to trail over the edge of the bowl and halfway down the pedestal. Low arrangements were sometimes tight tussie-mussies of mixed flowers and herbs, sometimes airy mounds of blossoms with their own foliage. Fruits and vegetables were heaped in shallow baskets or on round salvers.

Containers for flowers received unprecedented attention: fan-shaped vases, footed bowls, and apothecary jars were made of porcelain; tall vases, stemmed goblets, and cornucopias were of Venetian glass; gold and silver bowls and compotes were not uncommon, but, except in standing salt cellars, precious metals were most often used as mountings for other materials.

The Renaissance idea of numerous flowers in ornamental containers was the inspiration for eighteenth-century massed bouquets, and the Della Robbia wreath (interpreted in living materials) became a beloved, continuing Christmas tradition throughout the western world.

In the Elizabethan age, the England famed for brilliance of intellect and splendor of dress was notorious for the stench of her cities. Ladies followed the example of their queen and sniffed at nosegays as they walked or rode aboard. These were small bunches of sweet-scented flowers and aromatic herbs.

Elizabethan
Nosegays and Posies

In Elizabethan homes, posies (small tight bunches of a single variety of flower) in jugs were placed on tables and window sills. The tussie-mussie that combined perfumed flowers and sweet herbs was an indoor version of the nosegay.

The word *baroque* is said to come from the Portuguese "baroco," meaning an irregularly shaped pearl. The baroque style of the early seventeenth century made a fetish of asymmetry. Fruits, nuts, and berries (with their stems and leaves) were combined with flowers in huge S-curve arrangements. Pyramids of fruit, in tiered holders of porcelain or crystal, often decorated banquet tables. The walls of the most admired banquet halls were lined with niches holding busts; on state occasions, each arch was outlined with a garland, and each bust was crowned with a wreath. The effect was voluptuous and heavily graceful.

The Opulent
Asymmetry of Baroque

The seagoing Hollanders were famous traders and artisans. When the Dutch East India Company began to bring beautiful blue and white Nanking-ware from China, potters at Delft were quick to copy it. These cheaper imitations compared favorably with the oriental originals, and delft pottery was an instantaneous success. Massed bouquets in blue and white delft jugs and bowls were everyday decorations in palaces and in modest homes.

The rococo style that originated in France in the mid-seventeenth century was elegant rather than elephantine. *Rococo* meant "rock and shell," and the scallop-shell motif was omnipresent in carvings and in paintings. Asymmetrical flower arrangements were still in vogue, but the ponderous S-curve was shortened and lightened to a scrolled C, and then to a crescent. Flowers *and* arrangements were small; colors were delicate. Pastel blossoms might be combined with curved plumes in an ornamental porcelain urn; fan-shaped arrangements were made in finger vases. Miniature bouquets in minute vases were most appropriate for shapely white and gold tables in the Louis XV style. Ladies also carried hand bouquets, or wore small bunches of flowers in tiny "bosom-bottles."

The Delicate
Asymmetry of Rococo

In seventeenth-century America, wild flowers carpeted the forest floor in spring, and splashed their color across the hills in summer. Tree blossoms were succeeded by lush green leaves, and then by brilliant autumn foliage. In winter, evergreens bore comforting testimony of everlasting life. Of course, the native flowers, shrubs and trees differed somewhat from one colony to the next, and there was wide variance between the indigenous plants of northern New England and those of the far South. Englishwomen, however, were unanimous in their appreciation of whatever plant materials were at hand, bringing them indoors to enjoy.

FLOWER ARRANGING IN THE EARLY COLONIAL PERIOD

Flower gardens were established very early. Many a handful of seeds crossed the Atlantic in an apron pocket—not knowing what blossoming

33. *When Josiah Wedgwood established his pottery in England, in 1759, finger- and fan-shaped vases, boughpots, bowls, and tureens were in use as flower containers. The Wedgwood Pottery now reproduces in the original cream color this five-fingered Williamsburg posy holder, filled here in the eighteenth-century manner, with tall spikes of dock and grain interspersed with double larkspur and ragged robins; the arrangement has the look of a half-opened fan.*

plants they would find in the New World, women wanted to be sure of the solace of old favorites.

The settlers were far too busy building houses and furnishing them comfortably to be concerned with the difference between the baroque and rococo styles of flower arrangement. When the trailing arbutus and the wild sweet violets bloomed in New England, children must have gathered handfuls for their mothers, who arranged them, not in mugs or pitchers, which were reserved to their own specific uses, but in tygs. A tyg was a posy holder in three parts; a trio of small, squat, narrow-necked jugs, with linked handles, for short-stemmed flowers. In summer and fall, garden blooms were combined with field flowers in treen containers or clay-lined baskets.

To Nieuw Amsterdam, the Dutch brought delft flower jugs and bowls (the blue and white containers then in vogue in all of Europe) and their beloved tulips. To Philadelphia, the East India Company's ships that carried silks and spices from the Orient also brought tall vases and low bowls of ornamented porcelain. Contact with the Far East had taught Europeans that plant materials should be valued for their natural beauty and displayed in such a way that this beauty was emphasized. In the middle colonies, tree flowers—fuzzy maple buds, chestnut "hands," wild crabapple blossoms and angular branches starred with dogwood blooms—filled the tall vases of Chinese export ware. The South, trading directly with England, imported British-made flower containers along with English plants and seeds.

The shipment of plants across the ocean was a two-way exchange. The sciences of botany and horticulture were ascendant in Europe, stimulated by knowledge gained during the period of exploration, and new plant varieties from the colonies were avidly sought for experimentation. Goldenrod, a pesky weed to the settlers, was acclaimed in England as a valuable addition to the perennial border. On the other hand, the peony, which was disdained by European gardeners as too common, was eagerly welcomed by the colonists as a reminder of home.

In Georgian England (1714-1760), containers for flowers took on new forms. Wide-mouthed bowls and tall vases were being made by British potters in imitation of those imported from the Orient, and the tureen shape was increasingly popular. Blue and white china jugs and jars were produced in quantity, and called English delft; Holland's flower bricks were copied too. These were hollow china cubes, and their tops were perforated with several small holes surrounding one larger opening. Houseplants—especially geraniums begonias, and fuchsias—were used the year around as decorations; to make their containers as attractive as the plants themselves, designs for *cachepots* and wall pockets were borrowed from the French.

At this time, Grinling Gibbons' marvelous carved wooden wreaths, garlands and swags (each incorporating his trademark, a single pea pod) were widely copied in living materials. Flowers, fruits and foliage were combined with acorns, nuts, pods and cones. Fresh wreaths were made on circlets of metal, and garlands were supported by a core of rope.

The pineapple had become the symbol of hospitality. At Easter time, street vendors sold "pineapples" of clustered daffodil heads topped with their own spiky leaves. This traditional centerpiece for the Easter-morning breakfast table was easy to make: three flowers were encircled around several leaves, and tied in place with thread; a row of five daffodils was added and tied a little farther down the leaves, so close to the first row of blossoms that the petals touched and intermingled. Other rows were placed and tied, each a little fuller than the one above it, until the pineapple had

EIGHTEENTH-CENTURY BOUQUETS
Containers

34. *In the Baroque and Rococo periods, cornucopias were elaborately ornamented with asymmetrical designs. This cream-colored wall pocket, showing a figure in relief within a scrolled medallion frame, is now reproduced by Wedgwood from an eighteenth-century pair in the collection of Colonial Williamsburg. During the Classic Revival period, the cornucopia was in high favor, along with urns and amphora copied from Greek and Roman originals. Josiah Wedgwood learned to make a fine unglazed stoneware, and to decorate it in white relief with human figures, portrait busts, grapes, and acanthus leaves.*

attained the desired height and girth. Then all the stems were cut off even with the base. The pineapple would stand unsupported in a shallow water-filled saucer.

In summer and fall, it was the custom to fill each gaping fireplace with blossoms or greenery. Potted campanulas and monkshood were so universally used for this purpose that they were called "chimney flowers"; the plants were trained against miniature fan-shaped trellises of sticks. Branches of green leaves were massed in special containers called bough-pots, which were low, handled, wide-mouthed urns.

For obvious reasons, fashions in floral decorations arrived late in the colonies, but they lingered long. Throughout the eighteenth century, containers and arrangements of the Georgian period remained in favor, but earlier styles were not abandoned. In the Renaissance manner, tight tussie-mussies of mixed blossoms and single-flowered posies were used on tables and desks; in window embrasures, airy masses of flowers were enhanced by direct lighting. As for containers, tall beakers, boughpots, low-footed bowls and fan-shaped vases were popular, but holdovers from early colonial days were still in evidence: clay-lined baskets, treen ware, pewter, even gourd flasks and bowls. The Baroque period's delft pottery matched the prevailing blue-and-white color scheme dictated by the prevalence of indigo dye. For large arrangements, there were wide bowls—monteith (originally designed for punch) and Chinese export porcelain.

Plant Materials   An early traveler in North America was the Swedish botanist, Peter Kalm, for whom his friend and mentor Linnaeus named the showy mountain laurel *Kalmia latifolia.* He remarked that the English ladies of the provinces liked to have fresh flowers in their houses all summer long, and that they brought both wild and cultivated blossoms indoors.

Tree flowers that bloomed before the leaves put out lent themselves well to tall linear arrangements on deep window sills; late winter's witch hazel, wild plum and crabapple blossoms, fuzzy red and yellow maple blooms, pussy-willow catkins, and redbud's pink pea-flowered sprays were most effective when the angles or curves of their leafless branches were silhouetted against the light. Other tree blossoms (smoke-tree puffs, fringe-tree tassels, locust's silver bells or pink racemes, horse-chestnut candles, poplar's tulips) massed with their own foliage, became chimney flowers. After the blooms had faded, the leaves remained fresh in the boughpot for several weeks. In the South, *Magnolia grandiflora* with its huge sweet-scented blossoms and glossy deep-green leaves was preferred above all other plant materials for banking fireplaces.

Native blossoming shrubs were arranged alone or combined with flowers: rhododendron, mountain laurel, wild azalea, sweet shrub, mock orange, hydrangea, snowball, white spirea, highbush cranberry and mallow were particularly valued, either for their showy bloom or for their pleasant scent. There were native vines that helped to shape a graceful Hogarth curve or a crescent: honeysuckle (pink, white, red, and coral), white clematis, and wistaria.

All the delicate spring "wildlings" were sought out and placed in posy-jugs. Summer's taller wild flowers were combined in mass arrangements with blossoms from the garden; especially favored for this purpose were turk's cap and white spider lilies, wild roses, coreopsis, wild columbine, bleeding heart, black-eyed Susan, bee-balm, Queen Anne's lace, butterfly weed, false indigo (*Baptisia*), goldenrod, red clover, wild garlic, and wild asters. Its delicious perfume made nicotiana a highly prized pot plant; exported to England as a novelty, "flowering tobacco" became the rage in London, where it was proudly displayed on balconies and in shop windows.

The tulip was not the only bulb that was transplanted very early to American soil, but it remained a special favorite. Many colors and varieties bloomed in colonial gardens; even the showy parrot tulip was grown. The Dutch also brought hyacinths, scillas, and the early blooming crocus. The English imported their well-loved daffodils and narcissi (in particular, the vigorous *Narcissus poeticus*), the grape hyacinth, the tuberose, and the gladiolus. Gladioli were cultivated in a surprising range of color: pale and sulphur yellow, pale blue, flesh pink, deep red and deep purple.

The blooms of some herbs were included in flower arrangements—mint, for example, and both blue and scarlet sage. The nasturtium, however, was grown primarily as a seasoning; its petals and leaves were salad ingredients, and its seed pods were used as pickling spice.

Selling flower seed was an acceptable means of livelihood for women in colonial days. In March of 1760, this list appeared in an advertisement in the *Boston Evening Post*:

hollyhook, purple Stock, white Lewpins, Africans, blew Lewpins, candy-tuff, cyanus, wall-flower, pink, double larkinspur, venus navelwort, brompton flock, princess feather, balsam, sweet-scented pease, carnation, sweet williams, annual Stock, sweet feabus, yellow lewpins, sunflower, convolus minor, catch-fly, ten-week Stock, globe thistle, Globe amaranthus, nigella, love-lies-bleeding, casent hamen, polianthus, canterbury bells, carnation poppy, India pink, convolus major, Queen Margrets (asters)

All inclusive though it seems, this list does not offer the very popular marigolds, snapdragons, pansies, zinnias, lobelia, button chrysanthemums, sweet rocket, or the showy but smelly crown imperial. In addition to the globe amaranth and prince's feather mentioned, gardeners grew statice, artemisia, strawflowers, cockscomb and lunaria for winter bouquets. Peonies were for nostalgia, and no garden worthy of the name was without its roses.

With so multiple a choice of wild and garden blooms for cutting, it is not surprising that arrangements of fresh flowers were the most highly esteemed of all decorations for colonial homes. In most contemporary paintings, arrangements are shown as small tight posies, each composed of a single variety of flower, in low vases. Then as now, however, the realistic Dutch and English flower prints of the seventeenth and eighteenth centuries served as models for arrangers.

The much-admired floral decorations at Colonial Williamsburg often take their inspiration from a nurseryman's catalog of 1730. In that year, Robert Furbur of Kensington advertised his wares in an illustrated booklet, *Twelve Months of Flowers*. Each engraving showed various flowers that bloomed in England during a single month; included were some American varieties such as the goldenrod. The drawings were botanically accurate; each bloom was numbered and identified at the bottom of the print. The thing that set Robert Furber's catalogue apart from other plant listings was that his flowers were shown in massed arrangements.

Mechanics   The so-called eighteenth-century style in flower arranging was actually a matter of mechanics. Blossoms were clumped in jugs or tightly massed in bowls for mutual support—there was no such thing as a flower frog or a needlepoint holder. It was simple enough to crowd a few large blossoms or several smaller ones into a narrow-necked jug or a slender vase, and even simpler if their stems were first wrapped together with thread.

For window seats, branches of leaves, sprays of fruit blossoms, or bunches of long-stemmed flowers were naturalistically arrayed in tall vases of Chinese export ware, apothecary jars, or pewter beakers. Here mechanics dictated the choice of container, for it would have been wellnigh impossible to balance such heavy material in a bowl.

The full yet airy arrangement in a wide bowl or a tureen sometimes had no other support than the flowers could give each other. However, the bowl was often partially filled with sand or pebbles, and water was added. This served a dual purpose: to weight the container, and to anchor the flower stems. Fine gravel was usable only for woody stems, but sand worked well for all materials. Pebbles were also used in bough-pots, to hold the heavy plant stems securely. If necessary, the branches could be staked by tying them to short, sturdy sticks braced with larger stones against the side of the pot.

Finger vases, fan-shaped containers, and delft bricks were welcomed for the change of shape they made possible. Delft bricks were the most satisfactory of holders. Stems inserted through the holes in the top of the cube were supported midway between their ends and their flower heads. This meant that stiff, top-heavy hyacinths of graduated heights could be arranged in a spire. Branches of leaves or bunches of blossoms were steadied by the clustered holes; daffodils and tulips kept their place. If the arrangement was to be seen from all sides, it usually was built around a center of foliage placed in the large center hole.

A single flower or a posy in each aperture of a finger vase added up to an effective long and narrow composition. Finger vases doubled, too, as bulb planters. The vase was filled to the brim with water, and one dormant narcissus or hyacinth bulb was balanced in each flared opening. The vase was kept in a dark, cool place until the foliage sprouted, and then was brought forth and placed on a sunny window sill to force the blooms.

In fan-shaped vases, the outline of the arrangement followed the curve of the container's lip; for this reason, the background spikes or sprays were all cut to approximately the same length. The stems of foreground flowers were set in place at various angles to repeat the shape. Fan arrangements were preferred for fireplaces and wall niches, where their stylized effect was architecturally framed.

Directions

The tall, massed arrangement in a bowl or a tureen most often was placed on a table set against the wall, so it was flat at the back. The composition was large in proportion to the container, but not heavy—these full yet airy arrangements have been aptly dubbed "buxom bouquets." To reproduce the effect of an eighteenth-century mass bouquet, a tall, fan-shaped background of foliage or spiky flowers should first be set in place. The lowest wings, extending out from each side, level with the top of the bowl, should be as long as the tallest background spire. Then the front and sides of the arrangement should be built up of large blossoms of more than one variety, with regard to color harmony or contrast, but without a defined center of interest. Smaller blooms, short sprays of flowers, and foliage tips will serve as fillers, and should be added last. In order to have the arrangement quarter-spherical in shape, the flowers should lean toward the front of the bowl and should extend over the edge of the container for several inches.

For a free-standing mass composition, the background foliage or flower spikes should be placed first, in the shape of two crossed fans—front to back, and side to side. Spikes or sprays of flowers and foliage also should encircle the container at the lip; most of these should extend straight out at right angles, but some should curve downward very slightly. Then each of the four outlined triangles is built up with large blossoms and filled in with small flowers and shorter sprays of foliage.

Baskets were considered more appropriate than bowls for coarser garden blooms and field flowers; in order to keep the flowers fresh, the basket was given a clay bowl as a liner, and the bowl was filled with wet sand. Flowers were not really arranged in baskets, but merely massed for color. If blossoms are gathered up, two or three at a time, and thrust at random into sand, the effect will be right for a basket container.

FRUIT ON THE DINING TABLE

Incredible though it seems, flowers were not used on dining tables in colonial days. In the seventeenth century, the place of honor in the center of the table belonged to the standing saltcellar, of silver or pewter. Since it was the showpiece of the family tableware, the saltcellar was as large and as handsome as the breadwinner's purse allowed. Host and hostess, sharing a wooden trencher, sat side by side at the head of the table; guests,

35. *Early in the nineteenth century, glass bowls replaced silver dishes in American epergnes. By this time, fruit was for decoration; "dessert" had come to mean cakes, puddings, and ices. The White Hall Dining Room in the Museum of Early Southern Decorative Arts (from a house built about 1818 near Charleston, South Carolina) is furnished with graceful Sheraton and Hepplewhite pieces. Its silver and glass epergne has a large, shallow center bowl that holds an abundance of fruit; the three glass saucers are filled with candies and almonds. On the serving table, roses are arranged with their own foliage in a footed glass bowl.*

in the order of their importance, were seated along the sides, with children standing at the foot "below the salt."

By 1700, saltcellars had gone out of fashion, and had been replaced by *dormants*. These were platters of meat or poultry, used as decoration at one meal and eaten at another—for examples, a roast suckling pig with an apple in its mouth, or a pheasant, skinned, roasted, and returned to its plumage. In the 1740's, Eliza Pinckney wrote from South Carolina to a friend in England: *Dormants*

> The old silver, damask, and India china remaining show how these feasts were set out with the 'plateau' in the center of the table, of silver, glass, or china, the tall branching candlesticks, the two-handled loving cups (tankards, they called them) the heavy salvers with Queen Anne borders . . . Plenty of spoons they had, and two-pronged forks, but silver not . . .

By the time this letter was written, dormants on platters (plateaus) had been replaced by a centerpiece of fruits and nuts arranged in an epergne. Originally, fruit had been brought to the table as dessert, after the main course had been cleared away and the tablecloth removed. *Epergne* comes from the French "épargne," which means a sparing or a saving, and the epergne that remained on the table throughout the meal eliminated the serving of a separate dessert course by placing the fruits and nuts within reach of the diners. Eighteenth-century epergnes were of silver, and were used only in the more pretentious homes. A shallow bowl on a tall stand was surrounded by three or four smaller dishes supported by branching arms attached to the center pedestal at a lower level. Fruit often was used in all the containers, but sometimes a central dish of fruits was flanked by nuts and sweetmeats. *Epergnes*

In many homes, a handsome (empty) covered tureen served as a permanent centerpiece, a continuing vestige of the dormant.

Fresh fruit for the table in winter was not such a problem as might be supposed. In England, apples and pears had long been preserved by packing them in crocks between layers of dry moss. The jars were sealed with rosin, and buried in sand. The colonists soon learned, however, that all these precautions were unnecessary; apples and pears, as well as vegetables, kept through the winter in a root cellar. Bunches of grapes remained fresh for several months if they were carefully inbedded in sifted wood ashes; grapes also were dried in the sun, and the resulting clusters of raisins were served with nuts as a great delicacy. Watermelons and muskmelons were kept until Christmas time. The stems were broken off, and sealed at the break with a red hot poker; then the melons were stored in a cool, dark cellar. Lemons, a necessary ingredient of the colonists' favorite rum punch, had to be imported from the West Indies; they were dipped in wax to seal the rind and keep them juicy. The pineapple, traditional symbol of hospitality, also was imported from the islands, but because of its perishability was available only in seaport cities. *Keeping Fruits Fresh*

In season, the variety of fresh fruit was astonishing. Delicious berries of all kinds grew wild; for convenience, wild strawberries soon were transplanted to the kitchen garden where they responded to fertilization by growing much larger. Wild plums, crabapples, and grapes abounded; along *Fresh Fruits in Season*

the seashore, beach plums and cranberries grew rife. In the uplands persimmons, like miniature pumpkins, ripened with the first frost. To supplement these native delicacies, the colonists set out orchards of apple, peach, cherry, and pear trees, and planted figs and tender apricots against the kitchen chimney for protection against the winter cold.

The pomegranate, with its roots in history, was sorely missed by Englishmen in America; it had been used for centuries to decorate English churches and homes. Peter Collinson, a Quaker wool merchant of London who introduced many American plants to English gardens, wrote to his correspondent, John Bartram, in Philadelphia:

> Don't use the pomegranate inhospitably . . . but plant it against the south side of thy house, nail it close to the wall. In this manner it thrives wonderfully with us, and flowers beautifully, and bears fruit . . .

36. *The Classic Revival style was strongest in America in the first quarter of the nineteenth century; during this period, the epergne took on the shape of a tiered fountain. The lower bowl held fruit, but flowers were allowed to brim from the tall trumpet-shaped vase above it. In the dining room of Wellington House at Waterloo Village, New Jersey, a shallow crystal bowl rests on the short silver pedestal of the epergne; the flared crystal vase has a silver filigree base. Peaches and plums represent the traditional fruit in the lower container, while fresh roses and dried gypsophila are used in the trumpet vase and repeated in low china bowls on either side. On the mantel, a Wedgwood cachepot (dark blue, with raised white ornamentation) holds beech leaves and goldenrod.*

37. *As the Victorian era progressed, the epergne changed shape and left its fruit behind as it moved from the dining room into the parlor. Small, flared, slender vases replaced flat dishes in the center and on each branching arm; each container held a bouquet, and together they formed a pyramid of flowers. On the grand piano in the drawing room of the Seward House in Auburn, New York, a gilt and crystal epergne holds zinnias, asters, nasturtiums and snapdragons, with spires of blue salvia. On the opposite side of the music rack, long triangular glass prisms dangle from a gilded girandole with a marble base. This opulent house was built in 1817 by William Henry Seward, who became the first Whig governor of New York State (1839-43) and later served as Secretary of State under President Abraham Lincoln and his successor, President Andrew Johnson.*

John Bartram and many other colonial horticulturists followed this good advice, and espaliered not only pomegranates but also figs, peaches, and apricots on sunny south walls,

When glass became more common, a few persons of wealth solved the problem of out-of-season fruits and flowers with an *orangerie,* a small greenhouse built out from one wall of the house. As the name implies, orange, lemon, and lime trees could be grown there in huge wooden tubs, as could cherries, peaches, and apricots. Potted plants rested in the orangerie, and were brought into the house when they began to bloom; bulbs, started in dark cellars, were forced here, along with budded branches of fruit trees and shrubs.

In addition to being placed in epergnes on dinner tables, fruits were arranged in bowls, in compotes, and especially in baskets. The predominance of the basket-of-fruit motif in stenciling and embroidery would indicate that this was the way fruit customarily was displayed. In such designs, the basket usually was low, flared-oval in shape, and without handles. The fruit arrangement was balanced but not rigidly symmetrical. Apples, pears, and bunches of grapes with leaves and tendrils were constant components; cherries, peaches, and strawberries with their trilobed leaves were sometimes added.

ARRANGEMENTS OF THE CLASSIC REVIVAL PERIOD

In 1748, an Italian peasant tending his grapevines on the slopes of Mount Vesuvius came across traces of ancient ruins. This accidental find led to the excavation of the cities of Herculaneum and Pompeii, buried since 79 A.D. beneath pumice and volcanic ash. There was world-wide excitement over the discovery; as Pompeii was gradually unearthed, the simplicity, beauty, and comfort of its summer homes of wealthy Romans astounded architects and influenced their designs.

During the Classic Revival Period (1762-1830) fashions in flower arrangement followed the styles of furniture and architectural detail, in which the curves of the Baroque and Rococo periods had been replaced by straight lines and rigorous symmetry. Floral compositions were self-consciously geometric—pyramids, half-circles, ellipses—and the plant materials preferred in ancient Rome were once more in high favor: sheaves of wheat; ivy, oak, or laurel leaves; narcissi, jasmine, fruit blossoms, iris and poppies. Columnar and tripod pedestals held pale flowers in alabaster or bronze urns. Wedgwood urns, their blue, green or cream-colored backgrounds adorned with raised medallions, were contemporary adaptations of classic designs. Slim, flat wreaths and slender, ribbon–spiraled garlands were favorite decorative motifs in architecture and on furniture; these were repeated in living materials.

Figs and pomegranates replaced apples and pears in fruit arrangements, but grapes were, if anything, more popular than before. Fruit was mounded on flat baskets, or allowed to spill from tall Greek baskets and cornucopias.

During the Federal Period (1789-1801) the classic influence was not so all-important in the United States as in Europe. Boughpots and bowls of Chinese export ware were still the favorite containers. Bright flowers were still preferred. Silver epergnes continued to grace dining tables on state occasions, but tiered lustre or ceramic centerpieces were new and very popular. In them, for the first time, short-stemmed flowers were arranged with fruit.

The classic revival arrived full force in America during the first quarter of the nineteenth century. Columned porticoes led, through pedimented doors, to interiors furnished in classic style as interpreted by Duncan Phyfe. Marble table tops and pedestals held Wedgwood urns, prismed candelabra, or tole containers painted black and decorated with gold laurel wreaths. Mantels displayed matched sets of bronze or porcelain vases, girandoles, or lusters. Fashionable tables were centered with mirrored plateaus.

The most famous table decoration in all America was the magnificent *surtout de table* ordered from France in 1817 by President James Monroe. The principal piece is a plateau in seven sections, each twenty-four inches wide; altogether, the plateau is thirteen and a half feet long. The rim, which extends above the flat, mirrored inner surface, is decorated with garlands of fruit and flowers; at equidistant intervals, removable figurines of Bacchus and Bacchantes hold aloft crown candleholders and crystal vases for flowers. Made of bronze, the plateau was plated with silver when it was purchased. President Martin Van Buren ordered it gilded, along with the matching candelabra, compotes, and vases that complete the set, and bronze dore it has remained ever since.

Plateau

The Monroe *surtout de table,* used in the White House on all state occasions, set the fashion for table garnitures. American silversmiths made similar but smaller plateaus to order, adjusting their size to the tables on which they would be used. One or more epergnes or compotes sat upon the mirror, to be reflected in its surface, and were filled with fruit or flowers; candelabra were used on the plateau or at its ends. Often the compotes and candelabra were of porcelain rather than of silver.

By this time, the epergne had ceased to be a collection of small dishes surrounding a bowl-topped pedestal, and had taken on the classic shape of a tiered fountain. Its lower part was usually a footed bowl for fruit, surmounted by a trumpet-shaped vase for flowers. Silver was no longer the only acceptable material; epergnes began to be made of porcelain and crystal. As Victorian tastes prevailed over the classicism of the Early Republic, the glass epergne exceeded all other types in popularity. Gradually, short-stemmed blossoms replaced the fruit in the lower container, and flowers had arrived on the dinner table to stay.

Of course, not every household boasted a plateau or even a tiered epergne. Far more common (and very closely allied to the early-day concept of putting nothing on the table that was not meant to be eaten) was the large footed glass bowl with a domed cover that held honey or preserves. During the second half of the century, the inevitable everyday centerpiece was a caster. This was a stand, made of silver or Britannia ware, that held glass cruets and bottles containing condiments and spices.

VICTORIAN ARRANGEMENTS

At this time, dark red, dark green, brown and gold were the colors most often used for wallpaper, carpets and draperies; woodwork was dark, and varnished to a high shine. The Gothic Revival in architecture was reflected in tall chair backs, towering bed heads, and wood carvings that sought to imitate the stone sculpture of medieval churches. Against such a back-

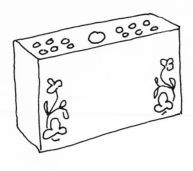

ground, flowers in shades of magenta, mulberry, ash-rose and lavender were most admired; mustard yellow, orange and dull-gold blooms were also popular. Instead of with their own leaves, flowers were arranged with serrated or plumy foliage. Ferns, palm fronds, and weeping-willow branches vied with plumed grasses in popularity.

Victorian ladies loved flowers, and had ample time to devote to them. They painted flowers on china, on glass or on velvet, embroidered them on canvas, molded them of wax, constructed them of shells and feathers, and even of human hair. Some of the blossoms they made looked only slightly less real than the ruffled, frilled and variegated flower forms they delighted to copy, the calceolarias, honeycomb dahlias, fritillarias and foxgloves that were crowded into hand-painted vases.

Meanwhile, the epergne had moved from dining room to parlor, and held flowers on the center table or on the piano. Hand-painted china vases stood empty on mantels and on side tables.

Repeating the "romantic" pseudo-Gothic style, flower arrangements featured weeping or trailing plant material. Fuchsias, freesias and bleeding hearts were prime favorites, along with the roses that were omnipresent in Victorian paintings, wallpapers, and textiles. The vases that held these flowers often were ornamented with raised decorations; the molded garlands or clusters of roses, cherubs, and shells were glazed and highly colored. It was not considered necessary that the flowers repeat the colors or the motif of the container. Most vases were modifications of earlier urn and cornucopia shapes; bulbous urns narrowed to stubby necks with slightly flaring rims, and china cornucopias were shortened and flattened almost to fan shape. A holdover from the Classic Revival Period was the tall ewer, with high-curved handle and down-flared lip, in bronze or porcelain.

The Victorians themselves were fond of saying that theirs was "the Age of Sentiment." They wore mourning brooches and crepe veils; they exchanged lace-paper valentines. They also revived the Elizabethan nosegay, edging it with a frill of lace, tying it with satin ribbon, and carrying it in a silver-filigree holder. They liked these hand bouquets so much that they made similar arrangements on flat saucers or in tall trumpet-shaped vases, and called them tussie-mussies. Around a single perfect rosebud, small flowers were placed in concentric circles—forget-me-nots, lilies of the valley, china asters, feverfew, tuberoses, button chrysanthemums or, most popular of all, huge deep purple Parma violets.

Wilful waste makes woeful want. In colonial America, this was no mere copybook maxim, it was a way of life. If each summer's abundance were not properly preserved for future use, any winter could become a "starving time."

Dehydrated foods are nothing new. At home, the colonists had eaten and liked smoked fish, and dried peas, beans and grains, and they had been accustomed to preserve meats and certain vegetables by pickling them in brine. From the Indians, they learned the principle of sun-drying, and found that when the shrivelled hardened foods were soaked and cooked in water they became plump again, and tasted almost fresh. Berries of all kinds, peeled and sliced fruits (apples, peaches, apricots and pears), green peas and shuck beans, slivers of pumpkin, and green corn kernels were spread out in a single layer on a sheet and placed in full sunlight and fresh air. Each night the sheet was bundled up and brought indoors. After two or three weeks, depending on their natural moisture content, the foods were ready to be stored until needed in gourds, crocks, or covered baskets.

Dehydrated Berries, Grains and Other Foods

Indians cut deer meat in thin strips and hung the slices over a grapevine stretched in the sun between two poles. This *pemmican* dried hard as leather, and could be carried by war parties or braves on hunting trips and chewed with a mouthful of water until it was soft enough to swallow. The colonists made pemmican, too, and found it very tasty when stewed all day until tender; by the same method, they dried thin slices of beef and called it "jerked beef," or "jerky."

To season their meat stews, the Indians used dried sweet and hot pepper pods and wild pepper grass. To these, the colonists added dried native and imported herbs: mint, sweet basil, bay-leaves, sorrel, thyme, dill, sage, and many others.

Dried Herbs

Doctors were few and far between, so every household had its store of dried medicinal herbs: horehound for cough syrup; boneset for a tea to help heal broken bones; plaintain for a poultice to draw infections to a head and to soothe insect stings; pennyroyal to be rubbed on the skin to discourage mosquito bites; feverfew to be steeped in water, to encourage sweating and thus break a fever; catnip and peppermint for colic; Joe-Pye weed (taking its name from an Indian medicine man) for general debility. Watermelon seed tea was used as a diuretic. A mixture of powdered rhubarb stalks and senna leaves provided a cathartic, and blackberry cordial controlled diarrhea. An infusion of sunflower seeds made a soothing eyewash. Sassafras root tea was a spring tonic, to "thin the blood."

Before they left their native land, the first settlers had known that herbs kept their strength best if tied in bunches and hung upside down in a warm room to dry. In England, they had dried certain flowers by this method, and used them all winter long for indoor decoration: cockscomb, prince's feather, salvia, artemisia, strawflowers, globe amaranth, and statice. Looking back on the early seventeenth century, Philip Miller wrote in his *Figures of Plants*:

> These flowers were formerly . . . cultivated . . . in the Gardens near London . . . and were brought to the Markets in great plenty during the Winter Season, to adorn Rooms. The Gardeners had a Method of staining them of a deep red and blue Colour, by dipping them into differen Liquids. So they brought them to the Markets in bunches of four Colours; white, purple, blue and red: And when their Stalks were put into Glasses with Sand, the Flowers would continue to Beauty until the Spring.

All over Europe, lunaria came to be prized for winter bouquets. When the brown outer husks and the seeds dropped away, clusters of thin translucent silvery circles remained on the dry stalks. Their resemblance to the full moon gave the plant its official title; they also looked like silver coins, and common names for lunaria were "honesty," "St. Peter's penny," and (in America after the Revolution) "silver dollar plant."

There was one strange new immortelle, pearly everlasting, that grew wild in great abundance in colonial America, and dried on its stalk to a mass of silvery beads. Women were delighted with it, and called it "life everlasting." Peter Kalm, the observant Swedish botanist and early-day tourist, wrote in his *Travels Into North America*:

> The English ladies gather great quantities of Life-everlasting, with long Stalks, and put them into pots with or without Water, with other fine Flowers from garden and field, placing them for an ornament in the Rooms.

Pearly everlasting was of attractive, clustered shape and had fine natural lustre, but it dried a disappointing greyish white. Colonial housewives, remembering the dyed statice and globe amaranth sold in the markets of English cities, soon were coloring it red, blue, and purple with madder, indigo, and a mixture of the two dyes.

To dried native and cultivated flowers, the settlers added sheaves of grain (wheat, oats and barley), corn and cane tassels and leaves, plumed grasses and sedge. For convenience, they hung their flowers and weeds to dry in windowless lofts—stripping off the leaves, tying the stems together in small bunches, and suspending them upside down from cane poles laid across the rafters—and discovered that blossoms dried in the dark kept their color exceptionally well. After a week or two, when the petals were dry and rather brittle to the touch, the "winter flowers" were ready to be arranged. Dried stems were thin and fragile, and needed to be handled with great care. Sometimes a tied bunch of short-stemmed blossoms, just as it came from the rafters, was placed in a posy jug or a gourd flask.

38. *Peter Collinson wrote of dried flowers as "a pleasant Ornament to Adorn the Windows of your parlor or study all the winter." On the wide sill of an open window with tiny diamond-shaped leaded glass panes, prince's feather, goldenrod, strawflowers and pearly everlasting are arranged in a tall blue and white delft jar. This typical seventeenth-century winter bouquet is in the Adam Thoroughgood House, property of the City of Norfolk, Virginia.*

39. *In the eighteenth century, many varieties of wild and cultivated plants were air-dried for winter bouquets. Some were tied in bunches and hung from the attic rafters. Others kept their shape better when placed upright in a sand-filled container. In the drying room at Colonial Williamsburg, a summertime harvest is readied for the arrangements that adorn the Governor's Palace, the George Wythe House, and the Brush-Everard House from November to March. Among the plants hanging from rafters and table are: Chinese lantern, dock, artemisia, strawflowers, feverfew, pearly everlasting, statice, yarrow, and globe amaranth. Drying upright are: cockscomb, plumed grasses, grains, cattails, and Queen Anne's lace.*

More often, however, the stems were carefully untied and several varieties of dried flowers, grains, grasses and seed pods were combined in an airy mass. A basket, a wooden bowl or goblet, a pewter beaker or a pottery jar might serve to hold the arrangement, but invariably the container was filled with sand. It was easy to set the shattery stems in place, and they stayed put.

When houses grew statelier and floral decorations more methodical in the eighteenth century, it was no longer considered sufficient to crowd as many dried flowers as possible in a sand-filled container. Winter bouquets were by no means abandoned; on the contrary, they were increasingly popular and elaborate.

EIGHTEENTH-CENTURY WINTER BOUQUETS

While Williamsburg, the capital of colonial Virginia, was at the height of its elegance and prestige, Peter Collinson (the London wool merchant and horticulturist) wrote to a friend there:

> If the flowers are gathered in perfection and hung with their Heads Downwards in a Dry Shady Room, they will keep their Colours for years and will make a pleasant Ornament to Adorn the Windows of your parlor or study all the Winter: I Dry great quantities for that purpose, and putt them in flower potts and China basons and they make a fine show . . .

Conditions for Drying Flowers

Many flowers dried successfully and kept their shape in the prescribed upside-down position, among them scarlet and blue salvia, butterfly weed, larkspur, gypsophila, feverfew, columbine, artemisia, stock, and snapdragons. But certain conditions had to be met if dried flowers were to retain their natural color. Perfect blossoms had to be selected, and picked the moment they reached maturity. (There were two exceptions to this rule: strawflowers, which had to be gathered before they were fully open to prevent browning of their centers, and Joe-Pye weed, which had to be cut in the bud stage in order to preserve its rosy-purple hue.) The flowers had to be gathered when their own moisture content was low, but not when leaves or petals were wilting—noon of a hot clear day was the ideal time—and hung at once without being placed in water. To prevent mildewing, no more than ten small stems were wrapped together in a bunch, and large stalks were hung singly. Light-colored blossoms were chosen for drying, since they held their true color; dark flowers tended to fade in streaks. The one absolutely essential requirement was a dry *dark* room in which to hang the blooms. Most flowers were ready for use in a week or ten days, when their petals were slightly brittle to the touch.

It was discovered that certain flowers changed color as they matured in field or garden. If they were cut at the desired color stage, further alteration could be arrested by drying. For example, the clustered heads of hydrangea, gathered at just the right moment, would retain their green, white, pale- or deep-pink tints; dock could keep the rosy tan of June, the wine red of July, or the mahogany brown of August; bamboo (*Polygonum cuspidatum*) held its first shell pink or its final crimson.

These flowers, however, drooped and tended to become amorphous masses when hung upside down—as did cockscomb, celosia, Queen Anne's lace, elder, goldenrod and lunaria—so they were dried right side up with their stems inserted in crocks or tightly woven baskets of dry sand. In fact, any flower with a stiff sturdy stem and a large composite head seemed to prefer

40. *Throughout the summer months, flowers and foliage are gathered from the meadows and gardens of Woodlawn Plantation by members of the Fort Belvoir Officers' Wives Garden Club, dried in clean white sand, and used in winter arrangements. In the Music Room, a pair of porcelain mantel vases that belonged to Nelly Custis Lewis are filled with oval arrangements in the Classic Revival style; the dried materials repeat the colors of the embroidered flowers on the firescreen panel.*

to remain vertical when brought indoors to the dark drying room. Plumed or heavy-headed grasses and weeds, placed in a perpendicular position with their stalks in sand, dried full and fluffy; bittersweet, wild heather, and Scotch broom retained their graceful curves.

Attractively shaped seed pods of some trees dried naturally to soft reds, *Air-dried Seed Pods* browns, and tans: sycamore balls; sweet gum stars; redbud's clusters of *and Foliage* slender pliant hulls; ghostly poplar tulips. Flower and vegetable seedpods, too, had interesting shapes, notably the unusual Chinese lantern, poppy, and okra forms. Milkweed and mullein, sumac and jimson were everywhere available for the gathering.

Certain types of foliage—galax, corn and rhubarb leaves, for instance— dried naturally on the plant. Others (mullein, iris and gladiolus) air-dried well if laid flat on paper in a darkened room. Still others could be air-dried on the branch, upright in a sand-filled container: *Magnolia grandiflora* and rhododendron which lightened as they dried to silvery sage green, red oak, white or silver-leafed poplar, and beech.

Any leaf was apt to wrinkle as it air-dried, or twist into a spiral or a *Pressed Foliage* cylinder. However, once they were thoroughly dehydrated, the leaves could be soaked in lukewarm water for a few minutes to make them supple again; they could then be smoothed with the fingers or flattened under a weighted board.

Pressing proved even more satisfactory than air-drying as a means of preserving foliage. Cinnamon and royal ferns, gathered as they approached maturity in late June, retained not only their soft green but also their pliability. Even the incandescence of autumn leaves could be captured and saved to brighten dark winter days, for pressed dogwood, maple, beech, hickory, red oak, sumac and sweet gum leaves responded well to this treatment. It was important to gather the leaves as soon as they attained bright color and before the sap had left the limbs, in order to prevent their falling off their twigs after they were dry. Straight branches were selected, and trimmed to lie perfectly flat; all overlapping leaves were snipped off. Then the branches were placed on the floor on three or four thicknesses of newspaper, and covered with more paper; planks were laid across these pads. For additional weight, bricks or heavy stones were ranged along the boards. As an alternative, the branches sandwiched between papers were placed underneath a chest with a flat base. In about three weeks, the foliage was ready to use, but women learned to leave it under weights an extra day or two; if any moisture remained in the leaves, their edges would curl when exposed to the air.

At Williamsburg, Virginia, the advice of Peter Collinson is followed to *Dried Arrangements* this good day. Magnificent masses of air-dried flowers and pressed autumn leaves adorn the rooms of the Governor's Palace, the Brush-Everard House and the George Wythe House from November until March, with time out for the traditional Christmas decorations. Miss Edna Pennell, who designs these much admired arrangements for Colonial Williamsburg, gives the following directions for making a "buxom bouquet":

> Fill the container with sand to give weight. For a low bowl, use a holder in the middle of the sand.
> Begin with a background of foliage, placing it in a fan-shaped outline. Use tall spikes of material, such as dried larkspur, to work out a design. If some of the spiked material is placed horizontally, the mass bouquet will gain added depth.

Fill in with other materials—dried goldenrod, baby's breath, or pearly everlasting. Add round weighty material, strawflowers perhaps, and work into a line of design within the mass silhouette.

Botany Prints

Throughout the eighteenth century, botanists from afar, like Swedish Peter Kalm and French André Michaux, explored American forests and mountains in search of new plant species. There was no camera to record their finds in natural color, no refrigeration to preserve berries or fruits for further study, and no quick and easy means of transportation to haul large live plants back to civilization. Naturalists took reams of notes, and filled sketchbooks with drawings; they gathered seeds, and dug roots for planting in botanical gardens; they managed to carry away specimen leaves, blossoms, and whole small plants by pressing them. Experiments in horticulture were by no means confined to the Old World. Many planters, including Thomas Jefferson, kept careful account of the life cycles of flowers as well as notes on the weather and records of crops, and there were serious scientists, like Philadelphia's John Bartram, who added much to the world's knowledge of horticulture. It was fashionable to take an interest in this subject that concerned the intellectuals of the day. The pressed specimens of returned explorers were examined and admired; soon they were imitated by amateur "botanizers" who found that pressed plants from the garden or the nearby woodland were ornamental as well as "philosophical." Framed panels of pressed flowers were much admired wall decorations.

The method of drying leaves and ferns by placing them between papers under a weighted board was applicable to flowers, but very often they were merely laid inside a folded sheet of paper and pressed between the pages of a heavy book—the family Bible, or Dr. Johnson's famous lexicon—for a week or two. It was not mandatory to select only naturally flat blossoms, like pansies, for pressing, but it was necessary to choose flowers with small calyxes that could be flattened without losing a clear and recognizable outline. Violets, pinks, columbine, larkspur, and bluebells were among the flowers that profiled to perfection. Some blooms kept their color exceedingly well while others did not. At a time when everlastings were colored as a matter of course, the solution was obvious: the bleached blossoms were dipped in dye and laid flat on paper to dry in the open air.

Mounting these thin and fragile pressed materials was an art in itself. The sturdiest specimens could have glue applied directly, with a soft brush, to their undersides and could be picked up by their stems (with the fingers or with tweezers) and transferred to mounting paper. Sometimes, however, pressed blossoms or stems would crumble under the pressure of tweezers or fingernails. In that case, glue was brushed on the mounting paper and allowed to stand until tacky. The flower was lifted with the moistened tip of a finger and gently laid on the sticky surface.

Small plants were very often treated as botanical specimens—dried intact and mounted to show the complete growth cycle: root, stem, leaf, flower and seed. Sometimes it was necessary that stems, leaves and even petals be pressed separately (and reassembled by gluing them individually) to obtain the desired naturalistic effect. The total colorful design, like a block print of the colonial period, was light and airy against a background of white. When the composition was complete, it was given a wooden backing and a narrow frame, and a protective glass that fitted flat against the glued materials to hold them securely in place.

Dried Flower Pictures

Dried flowers and dried or pressed foliage were as much admired for wall decorations as in arrangements, and when framed and glazed they were truly everlastings. It seems logical to assume that when a few blossoms and leaves emerged absolutely perfect from the drying room or from beneath the weighted plank, they were reserved for mounting on paper, cloth, or a wooden panel. For these a wreath design, a complete or an interrupted circle, was preferred. The outline of the design was drawn on the background and brushed with glue; while the glue still was wet, a background of foliage was laid in place and weighted with a heavy book to prevent curling of the leaf edges. A dried flower head had glue applied with a soft brush to its underside. It then was carefully picked up with tweezers or with the fingers and added to the flat wreath of foliage. Sometimes a few pressed flowers found a place in the composition. Since dried flower pictures were three-dimensional, they required deep frames that held the protective glass well away from the plant materials.

41. *This framed arrangement of dried and pressed materials, in the form of a classic wreath of victory, is from the collection of Waterloo Village. The flat sprigs of boxwood that form the background outline retain their deep green color after pressing. Superimposed dried flowers, cones, nuts, and berries make the composition three-dimensional.*

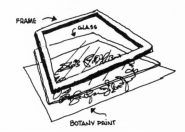

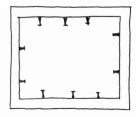

THE VICTORIAN ERA Victorian ladies preferred plumed grasses or truly permanent flowers made of feathers, wax, or shells to the immortelles that had brightened colonial homes in winter. Although they continued to press flowers between the pages of weighty tomes, they did so for sentiment's sake—to preserve a spray of lily of the valley from a bridal bouquet or a rose from a funeral wreath. Imprisoned in darkness for a century or more, these tender souvenirs emit a ghost of fragrance when the book is opened, and their colors still are bright against the printed page.

Potpourri A specialized use of dried flowers, for fragrance rather than for form and color, is *potpourri,* valued in England as an air-freshener since Elizabethan times. In the seventeenth and eighteenth centuries dried rose petals were scented in a covered jar with oils of rose, geranium, sandalwood, bergamot, and musk; orris roots and chips of sandalwood were buried in the mixture. When the lid was removed, concentrated scent rose from the jar to combat the fetid odors of a closed room.

In the colonies, where such esoteric ingredients were unobtainable, sun-dried flower petals (rose, lavender, geranium and verbena) were layered in a closed container or scattered over linens in a chest.

During the Victorian Era, potpourri of a different sort became very popular. It was made of dried rose petals and buds, in the old English manner, but powdered orris root and ground allspice, cinnamon and cloves were substituted for expensive oils and essences. For one pound of petals, two ounces of powdered orris was used, with one-half ounce of each spice.

Skeletonized Leaves The Victorians, who were so fond of Gothic architecture, managed to reduce leaves to their elemental architectural forms by a process called skeletonizing. To a quart of water, two tablespoonfuls of lye were added, and the mixture was brought to a boil in a porcelainized (graniteware) kettle. Leaves were immersed in the caustic liquid and simmered for forty minutes; then they were rinsed several times in cool water before being handled. A leaf was laid flat on a wooden breadboard, and with the dull edge of a tableknife all the fleshy pulp was carefully scraped away. This left a brown framework of veins, connected by a film of tissue so thin that it was very nearly transparent. To whiten it, the fragile leaf was soaked in buttermilk and bluing, and dried in the sun; then it was placed between sheets of paper and weighted with a heavy book for twenty-four hours, to flatten it. Skeletonized leaves were arranged with fresh flowers, or added to feather and wax compositions.

In the twentieth century, skeletonizing still is done by boiling leaves in a lye bath and scraping away the pulp with a dull knife, but blanching is easier. The leaves are soaked in a solution of household chlorine bleach: two tablespoonfuls of strong liquid bleach to one quart of water. One hour will produce a creamy beige color; two hours or longer will be required to turn the leaves completely white. When they are removed from the solution, they must be rinsed and dried between paper towels, and then pressed beneath a stack of books for twenty-four hours.

Ironing Leaves Late in the nineteenth century, students of botany were taught to preserve specimens for mounting by placing them between sheets of waxed paper (with a single sheet of brown paper, like a pressing cloth, on top) and ironing them with a hot sad-iron. Wax from the paper formed a thin

I. The kitchen was not only the heart of the colonial home, but also its craft workshop. This typical seventeenth-century fireplace, surrounded by the simple "conveniences" of the period, is in the well-equipped kitchen at the Old Museum Village of Smith's Clove. The Clove (from an ancient Saxon word meaning "valley") is located near Monroe, New York, in the valley of the Ramapo River, and settlement in the area dates from 1683. The Museum's comprehensive collection of tools and artifacts spans all periods of American craftsmanship from the seventeenth through the nineteenth centuries.

II. In the early nineteenth century, mourning pictures were made as memorials to family members and friends. The typical example (opposite), framed in black glass and inscribed in gold, has the customary grieving ladies in Empire dress, a monument urn, and weeping willow trees; the large anchor is the symbol of Christian Faith. It is from the collection of the Bartow-Pell Mansion, one of America's finest examples of Greek Revival architecture, which was completed in 1842. Late in the century it was purchased, with its extensive grounds, by the City of New York and became a part of the city's park system. In 1914, the restored house became the headquarters of the International Garden Club.

III. Murals by famous artists, itinerant painters, or talented family members decorated many an American wall in the eighteenth and early nineteenth centuries. The charming two-story President's Cottage at White Sulphur Springs, West Virginia, served as the Summer White House several times before 1850, and President John Tyler is said to have honeymooned here in secrecy with his bride. On the drawing-room walls (above), William C. Grauer's murals depict the resort in its heyday; over the mantel is The Old White, a famous hostelry from 1858 to 1922, the predecessor of The Greenbrier of today.

IV,V. At the Campbell-Whittlesey House in Rochester, N.Y. the Landmark Society has placed on display several very fine examples of painting on velvet (above). Theorem painting utilized stencils in a precise and orderly manner. Even the basket of fruit, so popular a design for embroidery and painted trays, was adapted to this mathematically exact method. There was a separate stencil for each component part of the design; stencils and directions for mixing paint and applying it to velvet were available from Theorem correspondence schools. Some gifted artists made lively and colorful freehand paintings on a yielding velvet surface. In the collection is a freehand painting of fruit and a basket (below).

VI. Homespun, a coarse material woven of the tow fibers combed out of flax in the process of making linen thread, was too scratchy to be used for clothing, so it was available for window curtains. At the Ship's Bottom Roof House in Saconesset (opposite), homespun curtains frame an arrangement of late-blooming October roses and pearly everlasting.

VII. In Plymouth, Massachusetts, the exhibits at the Harlow Old Fort House stress women's activities in the last quarter of the seventeenth century. Using old methods and ancient equipment, flax is prepared, spun and woven. The photo above left shows how the flax fibers on the spindle are twisted together by hand before being fed onto the small flax wheel which is turned by a foot treadle.

VIII. The Pilgrims made candles by dipping wicks, a rodful at a time, into a kettle of clear melted tallow. Candle dipping (above right) is demonstrated at Harlow Old Fort House, built in 1677 and now maintained by the Plymouth Antiquarian Society.

IX. The home built by Thomas Bowerman in 1678 at Saconesset, Massachusetts, is known as the Ship's Bottom Roof House, for the roof is bowed like the overturned hull of a seventeenth-century ship. Weaving was done in the spacious attic such a roofline provided, since colonial looms were too bulky to be kept in the family's living quarters. The basis of all cloth is a warp of taut parallel threads. The warping frame was first threaded and then laid flat on top of the loom. This partially threaded, very large frame held a forty-yard wrap—a tremendous length of cloth in colonial times.

X. From the earliest colonial days, American women decorated their homes with needlework so fine that it was in truth a form of art. In the eighteenth-century drawing room of the William Trent House in Trenton, New Jersey (opposite), a gilded mahogany pedestal firescreen graces the hearth. Its needlework panel still glows with color after two hundred years.

XI. In the collection of the Campbell-Whittlesey House in Rochester, New York is an eighteenth-century embroidered map of the world. The map (above left) is delicately worked on silk; the four embroidered pictures within the oval are miniature landscapes with figures of American Indians.

XII. The colorful block-patterned quilt top (above right) was pieced by President Calvin Coolidge in 1882, when he was ten years old. Vermont winters were long, and it was not unusual for boys as well as girls to be kept quiet and occupied with simple sewing. In later years, Mrs. Coolidge assembled the blocks, but did not add batting or lining. The quilt is displayed upon the bed in which the President was born, at the Coolidge Homestead in Plymouth Notch, Vermont.

XIII. The best-known and best-loved of all eighteenth-century arrangements is the "buxom bouquet" (below). This tureen-shaped, white porcelain bowl holds white spirea; white lilac; white, pink, yellow and red tulips; white and pink azaleas; narcissi; single hyacinths and pansies. The Craighead-Jackson House, built in Knoxville, Tennessee, in 1818, is the setting for this arrangement. In 1967, restored by the Blount Mansion Association, it was opened to the public. The garden is maintained, and flower arrangements for the house are furnished, by the Garden Study Club.

XIV. Before 1650, Adam Thoroughgood built a sturdy brick house that is now the property of the City of Norfolk, Virginia. On a carved oak Jacobean chest (opposite), a bowl of celosia, cockscomb, statice and strawflowers has sprays of grass and grain for airiness and Chinese lantern pods for interesting contrast of shape and color. The arrangement, placed in front of a spice chest, is flanked by tall wrought-iron candleholders.

XV. The translucent, silvery circles of lunaria (opposite) earned it the common names of "honesty," "St. Peter's penny," and "silver dollar plant." In Europe and America, it was the most admired of winter decorations; this arrangement, with polygonum, in a blue-and-white Chinese bowl, makes lunaria's popularity easy to understand. It is in the Adam Thoroughgood House, Norfolk, Virginia.

XVI. On the early eighteenth-century lacquered and gilded tea table in the drawing room of the William Trent House in Trenton, New Jersey, a colorful rounded arrangement combines globe amaranth, strawflowers, and statice with dyed everlastings in a footed pewter bowl (above left). A pewter teapot and fluted tea china complete the setting.

XVII. At the Blount Mansion, in Knoxville, Tennessee (above right), pale pink rhododendron is massed with dark red tulips in an English delft vase. On the table, a shagreen case holds a pair of gentleman's silver shoe buckles. The Mansion, built in 1792 by Governor William Blount, served as the capitol of the Territory South of the River Ohio.

XVIII. Stuffed birds were much admired as a decoration throughout the nineteenth century. On the Empire style console table (above) in the President's Cottage at White Sulphur Springs, West Virginia, a quail, a parrot, a bluebird and a redstart take shelter together under a tall glass dome. Over the table are pictures of four of the seventeen Presidents of the United States who have visited White Sulphur Springs. Only eight actually stayed in the President's Cottage; these, all in office before the Civil War, were: Jackson, Van Buren, Tyler, Polk, Taylor, Fillmore, Pierce, and Buchanan.

XIX. In the spacious formal parlor of the mid-nineteenth century Tallman House at Janesville, Wisconsin, an arrangement of wax flowers under glass (opposite) occupies a place of honor on the draped center table. This setting typifies the comfort and charm of the Victorian era in America: patterned carpet, velvet-covered chairs, a marble bust upon a pedestal, heavy gold frames for pictures and mirrors, gaslight, and music in the home. Abraham Lincoln was the weekend guest of William Tallman here in 1859.

XX. Ornamental gourds were grown especially for decoration in colonial times. In the Blount Mansion kitchen (above), several varieties are heaped in a copper basin and topped with one small ear of strawberry corn. Behind the gourd arrangement is a breadboard.

XXI. In a beautiful Chinese bowl, a glowing arrangement made by Mrs. Georgia S. Vance brightens the James Monroe Room, Diplomatic Reception Suite of the Department of State, Washington, D. C. The smallest flowers were air-dried; larger blooms (zinnias and lilies) were preserved in sifted sand. The unbelievably lifelike roses were cured in silica gel.

XXII. In the dining room of the Trent House, a dried arrangement on the sideboard (above right) complements the crimson velvet upholstery of a tall carved oak chair. A blue and white delft vase, made in Holland about 1700, holds strawflowers, zinnias and larkspur, with a fan-shaped background of pressed ferns. The Garden Club of Trenton, New Jersey, annually provides winter arrangements suited to the furnishings of the house.

XXIII. Wood was the most available of materials in all the colonies, and treen ware was all-important in the early settlers' homes—before 1700, every dinner table was set with wooden trenchers and cups. In the seventeenth century Ship's Bottom Roof House at Saconesset, Massachusetts, a window with homespun curtains sheds its light on a treen candleholder and a maple burl bowl (opposite). A split basket in the background holds a typical winter bouquet of dried grasses and everlastings gathered in nearby fields.

XXIV. Peppers came, like Joseph's coat, in many colors, and a garland that included yellow, orange, red and brown hung all winter long on the chimney in the separate kitchen building at the Blount Mansion in Knoxville (below). The string of red hot-peppers at one side of the fireplace was used as needed for seasoning. Dried sage is feathery but colorless; to make it more decorative, it often was tied with bright dyed yarn.

XXV. In the eighteenth century, boxes of all sizes were covered with colorful paper; the smallest scraps of wallpaper were carefully saved for this purpose. In addition, hand-printed paper, in small overall designs, decorated the outside and the inside of hat- and bandboxes. Throughout the nineteenth century, trunks often were lined with pasted newspaper. At the Saconesset Homestead, the Museum Shop offers reproductions of two document boxes (above), covered with early nineteenth-century wallpaper, and lined with newspapers from the 1870's.

XXVI. While waiting to be cooked, squash added a cheerful splash of color against pine-paneled walls (above). In the separate kitchen building of Blount Mansion in Knoxville, yellow crooknecks rise above pattypan squash and parsley in a lacy honeysuckle basket. Beside the arrangement is a horn cup, with silver rim and monogrammed disk.

XXVII. With a little artistic ability, considerable imagination, and a very sharp knife, a man could create many useful articles that were decorative as well. Two hand-carved butter molds and a stick stamp are displayed (opposite below) on a mat of homespun material dyed with onion skins. The eighteenth-century square mold with twin-star pattern holds approximately one pound of butter; the round nineteenth-century mold has a much more intricate sheaf-of-wheat design and makes a half-pound pat. The inch-wide stick stamp has an incised acorn motif; such stamps were used for printing small allover designs or borders on cloth or paper.

XXVIII. The Adam Thoroughgood House, near Norfolk, has been called "the archetype of the small seventeeth-century Virginian farmhouse." In this house, as in other contemporary homes throughout the southern colonies, the traditional English Christmas was observed. Wreaths and garlands decorated the fireplace wall above the burning yule log. The evergreen wreath shown (opposite) has small red crabapples and yellow Seckel pears added in the della Robbia manner. The bright-red berries of holly and yaupon set the scene for feasting, and merriment around the punchbowl. Fruits, and especially red apples, were carefully preserved for holiday enjoyment.

XXIX. In the deep cellar of the Brother's House in restored Old Salem, at Winston-Salem, North Carolina, a large Nativity scene is set up each year. It shows the town of Bethlehem and the surrounding countryside as they might have appeared on the night of Christ's birth. In the view above, the Three Wise Men, garbed in richly ornamented flowing robes, approach the manger across the desert sands.

XXX. A second portion of the Nativity scene at the Brother's House in Old Salem shows the Manger, in a stable that was in reality a cave. Long ago the Moravian residents of the Brother's House carved and painted the figures of the Holy Family and the sheperds, and added sheep and domestic animals. While the putz is on display, an annual Candle Tea marks the opening of the Christmas season in Winston-Salem. The making of beeswax-and-tallow candles is demonstrated; traditionally, each is trimmed at Christmas with a ruff of red paper near the base.

protective coating on both sides of the leaves, which could be lifted as soon as they were cool and dried overnight between the pages of a heavy textbook. This trick works well for coleus, hosta, scarlet maple, gingkho and caladium leaves (which do not respond well to other methods of preservation) and may also be applied to green grasses and tiny wild flowers. An electric dry-iron should be used, at the setting for synthetic materials.

Of late, the pendulum of preference has swung back to immortelles. Air-drying (upside down or right-side up) and pressing still are considered by many purists the best ways to deal with plant materials, but newer methods of preserving flowers and foliage for color have their ardent advocates. Massed in bouffant bouquets, these new "cured" blossoms have the just-picked look of a fresh flower arrangement in the eighteenth-century manner, and their lasting qualities are a boon to the many garden-club members who take on the responsibility of providing appropriate period floral decorations for historic-house museums.

Creative thinkers discovered that many flowers resistant to all efforts to air-dry them successfully could be preserved in perfection of shape and glory of color by burying them for a period of time in absorptive granular material. Sand, which had been proven harmless to the stems of flowers dried in an upright position, was first used for this purpose, and still is preferred by many talented arrangers of dried materials.

Clean, dry sifted sand or marble dust is placed in a heavy cardboard box at least six-inches deep. (Sand from the seashore must be soaked in fresh water, rinsed, and dried in the oven to remove salt and other minerals that affect color.)

Cut the flowers with short stems. Do this at the driest time of the day, when no dew is on the petals; wait two days after a heavy rain.

Clip the stem close to the head of the blossom, and insert heavy green florist's wire (number 18) into the cut end, pushing the tip of the wire up through the hard green calyx to emerge in the center of the bloom; bend the wire tip in a miniature shepherd's crook, and pull on the wire stem until the point of the crook disappears into the calyx. (As the flower dehydrates, it grips this foreign object tighter and tighter, and clings to its wire stem when thoroughly dry.) Bend the wire at right angles, an inch below the flower head.

Place a two-inch layer of sifted sand in the bottom of the box. Scoop a shallow depression in the sand, and settle the flower carefully in it, face up, with the bent stem imbedded below the surface of the sand to help hold the flower steady. With the fingers, push sand up and around the edges of the flower, so that the outer petals are held in their natural position. Then trickle a thin stream of sand over the inner petals and the center of the blossom. Add sufficient sand to cover the flower to a depth of one inch.

These directions apply to roses, carnations, small dahlias, gladiolus florets, hollyhock blossoms, and button chrysanthemums. In hot, dry weather, roses dehydrate in sand in about four days; if an inner petal feels crisp, the flower is ready to be removed. Half-open roses respond better to this treatment than do buds or full-blown blossoms.

Larkspur, delphinium and snapdragons (with fine florist's wire pushed up through their own hollow stems for reinforcement) should be laid

TWENTIETH-
CENTURY
TECHNIQUES FOR
PRESERVING PLANTS

Sand Drying

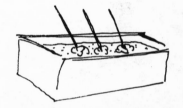

horizontal in a shallow trough of sand, and then covered completely.

Straight-petalled zinnias, wired through the calyx, should be placed face down on the sand and gently moved from side to side until partially imbedded. Then sand is sifted over the back of the flower to a depth of one inch. This position is best for daisies, black-eyed Susans, Korean chrysanthemums and sunflowers, and works well also for ageratum and ragged robins *(Lychnis)*.

Small sprays of rose leaves or ivy may be sand dried by laying them flat on the surface of the deep lower layer and covering them with an additional one and a half inches. They require a longer drying time than flowers, from ten days to two weeks.

Cornmeal and Borax   Many people prefer to substitute for sand a lighter mixture of five pounds bolted yellow cornmeal and fifteen ounces of powdered borax (one large box of borax, as sold in supermarkets.) Any topless wooden, cardboard, or plastic container may be used, but not a metal one. Only one inch of the borax mixture is needed in the bottom of the box; it is not necessary to add a thick top layer, but it is imperative that each flower be completely covered. The same directions for adding wire stems and positioning the blossoms apply, and roses should be ready for use in approximately one week. All the particles of the drying agent should be gently flicked away with a soft artist's brush. If the borax and meal mixture is dried for an hour in the oven at 150°, and stored in an airtight container, it may be used again.

Green beech leaves dry faultlessly in cornmeal in about two weeks. Meadow rue and ferns preserved in this way are more natural in appearance than pressed specimens, since they retain slight irregularities of edge and natural curves. Sprays of white flowering dogwood (face up) dry to perfection in about two weeks, but pink dogwood blossoms do not keep their true color. (Wild flowering dogwood is protected in most states by stringent conservation laws, and the blossoms may not be cut or sold. Lawn specimens, however, often are shaped by judicious pruning, which may be done while the trees are in bloom.)

Silica Gel   Newest of the granular drying agents is silica gel, which is obtainable through a florist. It looks not unlike sand, but has a great many small blue crystals. As these crystals absorb moisture from dehydrating flowers (or from the air) they turn pink; if the gel is placed in the oven at 150°, it can be dried for re-use, and is ready when the crystals have regained their original blue.

This method of preservation works best for fully open flowers—tight centers and buds dry hard and brown. The flowers are placed face up, on a two-inch layer of the gel in an open box, and covered to a depth of one inch. It is, of course, important that only one layer of flowers be in the container, so it is advisable to use a large flat cardboard box—a dress box rather than a carton from the grocer.

As always, there are exceptions to the rule. Hollyhock, single althea, and gladiolus florets, mallow and hibiscus blossoms, and large daffodils should be dried face down. The gel is mounded to support the inner surface of the flower, which is fitted over this heap and then covered very gradually so as not to break the edges of the petals. Azaleas dry beautifully in silica, as do rhododendrons, but for these a smaller, deeper container must be used. Once the cluster is in place on a two-inch layer, gel must be added very gradually and carefully mounded over each floret to prevent crushing and crumpling of petals. Lilacs not only keep their shape and color when dried upright in this manner in a deep box, but also retain their fragrance!

Flowers cure more rapidly in silica gel than in other granular materials, and should be checked at the end of the third day. When ready for use, their petals are silky rather than crisp or brittle to the touch.

Cured flowers may be stored until needed (in florist or dress boxes) in a windowless closet; hanging a cake of dehumidifier in the closet is an advisable precaution. Once arranged, the dried materials must still be protected from dampness and strong light. In a house with year-round air conditioning, where temperature and moisture are controlled, they will last for several years. Placed before an open window on a rainy day, they wilt almost immediately.

Glycerin Method

Flower arrangers feel that even the best sprays of pressed leaves have one great disadvantage: they are perfectly flat. In glycerin, chemistry has provided a new dimension in the preservation of broadleafed evergreen foliage. Rhododendron, magnolia, eleagnus, scotch broom, laurel, and holly respond especially well to this method, which is exceedingly simple.

Late summer is the best time to treat evergreen leaves, after the new-growth tips have become woody. The branches should not be cut when the leaves are wilted by a prolonged drought, but should be gathered on a clear, hot day; for best results, the sprays should be no more than twenty-four inches long. Clean the leaves by wiping them with a wad of cotton dipped in glycerin or salad oil. Then strip four inches of bark from the bottom of the stems, and cross-split the stem ends. In a tall slender container (an old florist's vase or a quart milk bottle) place one cup of glycerin (from the drug store); add two cups of boiling water, and stir vigorously with a long-handled spoon until well mixed. While the mixture still is hot, plunge the stems into it, making sure than their scraped ends are completely covered. Keep the container where it will be seen daily. It is interesting to watch the leaves change color as the glycerin slowly seeps along their veins. The branches should be removed from the solution as soon as the color change has reached the edges of the top leaves; this full absorption usually takes place in about five days. Rhododendron leaves take on a deep bronze sheen, and magnolia turns milk-chocolate brown. To keep a green tinge, leave the foliage in the glycerin mix for two days only; then hang it upside down in a dark attic or closet for three more days to complete the curing process.

Some deciduous foliages—oak and beech leaves in particular—turn greenish brown in glycerin. Dogwood foliage flouts all rules by taking on a deeper, richer green; it must remain in the glycerin solution two full weeks to be permanently preserved.

Galax leaves, ivy and vinca minor sprays, and boxwood or azalea twigs are treated by submerging them in a mixture of equal parts glycerin and water. This should be done in a flat, shallow container—an oblong roasting pan is ideal—and the leaves should be weighted with small clean stones to keep them beneath the surface at all times. Ivy takes on a deeper green, and is ready for use in six days. Galax turns mahogany red in ten days. Other materials turn brown when completely cured.

Wrinkled air-dried or glycerin-treated leaves may be smoothed with an electric dry iron set for synthetic materials, using one sheet of waxed paper plus one layer of newspaper as a pressing "cloth."

Preserving Berries   In its various shades of brown, glycerined foliage is extremely attractive when arranged with fall flowers and bright autumn berries, but berries may shatter before chrysanthemums fade. Here again, chemistry provides a solution to the problem: berry sprays may be dipped into a mixture of equal parts white shellac and alcohol, in a shallow roasting pan protected by a liner of heavy-duty aluminum foil. The thinned shellac is very nearly invisible on berries and stems, and works well on bittersweet, nandina, bayberry, and privet, and on magnolia pods, keeping their bright red seeds in place for weeks. Vitex and liriope seed stalks retain their beaded look. Such fleshy berries as pyracantha, honeysuckle, eleagnus and mahonia will not be permanently preserved, but their house-life will be greatly lengthened. Cat-tails may be kept at any color stage—green, beige, or brown—by thorough dipping, and the shellac coating will keep them from explosively shattering.

Some small, fragile berries and some shattery dried flowers (calicarpa berries, for instance, and polygonum) do not respond well to dipping in shellac; they glue themselves together in shapeless masses. These may be sprayed with colorless acrylic plastic, which is available in pressurized cans at paint stores and is cheaper and less noticeable than hair-spray.

Pressed Flowers   No method has completely replaced pressing for preserving green leaves
and Foliage   and ferns, and colorful autumn foliage. For contrast in shape, the interesting serrated leaves of butterfly bush, peony, poppy, and vitex have been added to the pressing list. On a hard, unyielding surface (the floor, or a table) the material is laid flat on four thicknesses of newspaper and covered with four more. If space permits, the paper-covered foliage should be topped with planks or a sheet of wallboard and weighted with bricks, books, or heavy stones. It can, however, be tucked under the rug in a passageway or a room where foot traffic is heavy; it could be placed between the box spring and the mattress of a bed.

Since fresh flowers and their stems contain much more moisture than tree foliage or ferns, they cannot be placed under weights and ignored for a fortnight. Twentieth-century pressed-flower enthusiasts fold blossoms (or even entire plants, complete with roots) inside four sheets of newspaper, weighting them with a stack of books instead of with board and bricks. For the first two days, the newspapers should be changed every twelve hours; after that, fresh papers are needed once a day. Depending upon the fleshiness of petals and stems, the pressing process is complete in eight to ten days, when the petals look and feel dry.

Pressed-flower panels, in eighteenth-century designs, are produced commercially; in them the colors of the flowers are reinforced with dyes. Amateur craftsmen nowadays prefer the realism of natural color, but find that after about two years most red and blue blossoms have faded to pallid lavender or gray. Light rather than air is the enemy of color in pressed-flower pictures; they should never be exposed to direct sunlight.

In the Southern Appalachian region, women still gather wild everlastings and dye them for winter bouquets. The dyes are no longer limited to the indigo blue and madder rose used in the seventeenth century to color statice and globe amaranth; yarrow, pepper grass, and pearly everlasting are sold in a veritable rainbow of colors. Liquid dye is diluted with boiling water to the desired shade; the flower is held by the stem and dipped carefully into the infusion so that only the flower head is submerged, lifted and shaken over the dye-pot to remove any excess that might stain the stems. The stalks are placed upright, in sand-filled buckets, to dry, and spaced so that the blossoms do not touch. Appalachian craftswomen buy only red, blue, and yellow dyes, and achieve a wide range of colors by mixing them.

Dyed Everlastings

42. *In the eighteenth century, whole plants—roots, stems, leaves, and blossoms—were pressed and framed, perhaps an outgrowth of contemporary interest in botany. Colonial-style pressed-flower panels, preserved under glass and given characteristically narrow frames, are reproduced from originals in the collection of historic houses; many of these use artificially-colored pressed materials, to overcome the problem of fading, and this was customary in colonial times. These three panels are from the Williamsburg Collection at B. Altman and Company, New York.*

METHODS OF PRESERVING FLOWERS AND FOLIAGE

Ageratum	Cure face down in silica gel
Alder cones	Cut green, air-dry upright
Allium (onion, garlic)	Air-dry, hanging upside down
Amaranth	Air-dry hanging
Artemisia	Air-dry hanging
Astilbe	Air-dry right side up
Azalea	Right side up in silica gel, deep box
Baby's breath	Air-dry hanging, by single stalks
Baptisia	Blue-black seed pods dry on stalk; dip in shellac and alcohol
Bayberry	Dip in thinned shellac
Beauty-berry (Callicarpa)	Dip small bunches in thinned shellac, spray long wands with acrylic plastic
Beech leaves	Press, air-dry upright, or treat with glycerin
Bittersweet berries	Dry naturally on vine, or air-dry upright; dip in thinned shellac
Black-eyed Susan	Face down in sand or cornmeal-borax
Bluebell	Press; cure horizontal in silica gel, reinforce stem with wire
Boxwood	Submerge twigs in glycerin
Butterfly-weed (Asclepias tuberosa)	Air-dry right side up; cornmeal-borax
Caladium leaves	Iron between sheets of waxed paper
Carnation	Cornmeal-borax; silica gel
Cat-tail	Cut before fully ripe. Air-dry upright; dip in thinned shellac
Celosia	Air-dry, right side up
Chinese lantern (ground cherry)	Air-dry hanging
Chrysanthemum	Silica gel
Cockscomb	Air-dry, right side up
Coleus	Iron leaves between sheets of waxed paper
Columbine	Silica gel
Corn leaves and husks	Dry naturally on stalk; soak in lukewarm water to shape
Corn tassels	Dry naturally, or air-dry upright
Daffodil	Upside down in silica gel or cornmeal-borax
Dahlia	Silica-gel, cornmeal-borax, sand
Daisy	Cornmeal-borax, silica gel, sand
Dock	Cut at right time for color (green in spring, rose in summer) air-dry upright
Dogwood blossoms	Cornmeal-borax
Dogwood foliage	Turns dark green in glycerin (two weeks)
Elder flowers	Silica gel
Eleagnus	Treat foliage with glycerin; dip berries in thinned shellac
Eucalyptus	Air-dries in arrangement, no treatment
Euonymus berries	Dip in thinned shellac
Euonymus foliage	Stand shrub branches in glycerin; submerge sprays of climbing and trailing varieties in glycerin
Ferns	Press, or dry in cornmeal-borax
Feverfew	Air-dry hanging; cornmeal-borax
Galax	Press, or submerge in glycerin
Geranium	Upright in silica gel, deep box

Ginkgo foliage	Press; iron individual leaves between sheets of waxed paper
Gladiolus florets	Upside down in silica gel
Gladiolus leaves	Air-dry flat, on paper
Globe amaranth	Air-dry hanging
Globe thistle	Cut before fully open, leave top leaves on, air-dry hanging
Goldenrod	Cut before upper florets open; air-dry right side up
Gourds	Pierce both ends; dry on paper, turning daily and wiping away moisture
Heather	Dries naturally in arrangement; color better if air-dried hanging
Hibiscus (and Mallow)	Cure individual florets upside down, in silica gel
Hickory foliage	Press or cure in cornmeal-borax
Holly	Treat foliage in glycerin; spray berries with acrylic plastic
Hollyhock (and Althea)	Cure individual flowers upside down, in silica gel
Hosta	Iron between sheets of waxed paper
Honeysuckle berries	Dip in thinned shellac
Huckleberry foliage	Air-dry, press, or treat with glycerin
Hydrangea	Pick for desired color (pale green, white, pink, dusty rose); air-dry upright
Iris	Cure individual blooms in silica gel; air-dry foliage flat, on paper
Ivy	Cure in cornmeal-borax, or submerge in glycerin (six days)
Joe-Pye Weed . . . . (*Eupatorium purpureum*)	Cut just before buds open to retain color; hang single stalks to air-dry
Larkspur (and delphinium)	Cure horizontal, in silica gel
Laurel foliage	Treat with glycerin
Liatris	Air-dry hanging
Lilac	Upright in silica gel, deep box
Liriope	Press foliage; dip seed stalks in thinned shellac
Lunaria (Honesty)	Cut after seed pods mature, air-dry upright, peel off husks and seeds
Mahonia	Dip berries in thinned shellac; treat foliage with glycerin
Magnolia foliage	Glycerin mixture: two days for green, then air-dry hanging; ten days for brown
Magnolia pods	Dip in thinned shellac to retain seeds
Maple foliage	Press, or cure in cornmeal-borax
Marigold	Sand, cornmeal-borax, silica gel
Meadow rue	Cornmeal-borax
Milkweed pods (*Asclepias*)	Cut green, split to remove silk; air-dry hanging (sage green outside, yellow within)
Mullein	Gray rosettes dry naturally in field
Nandina	Dip berries in thinned shellac; iron leaves between sheets of waxed paper
Narcissi	Silica gel, cornmeal-borax, sand
Oak leaves	Press, air-dry, or treat with glycerin
Okra pods	Air-dry, upright or hanging
Pampas grass	Cut when fluffiest, arrange without water
Pansy	Press; cure in silica gel

Pearly Everlasting	Cut just before maturity; air-dry hanging
Peony	Silica gel. Single varieties cure best
Pink	Cornmeal-borax, silica gel
Polygonum (bamboo, knot-bush)	Cut as soon as tiny flowers turn red; strip leaves, arrange at once, then spray with acrylic plastic
Pomegranate	Pierce both ends; dry on paper in dark room; turn daily, wipe away moisture
Poplar alba (silver-leaf)	Air-dry right side up, or cure in cornmeal and borax
Poppy	Press leaves; cure flowers in silica gel
Privet berries	Dry dark blue on bush, or cut green, dry hanging. Dip in thinned shellac
Pyracantha berries	Dip in thinned shellac or spray with acrylic plastic
Pussy-willow	Curve with fingers when freshly cut; arrange without water. No treatment
Queen Anne's lace	Silica gel, cornmeal-borax
Ragged robin	Cornmeal-borax, silica gel, sand—face down
Rhododendron flower	Right side up in silica gel, deep box
Rhododendron foliage	Air-dry upright; treat with glycerin
Rhubarb foliage	Air-dries on plant
Rose	Silica gel, cornmeal-borax
Rose foliage	Press, or cure in sand, cornmeal-borax
Salvia (red or blue)	Cut fully matured. Air-dry hanging, or cure horizontal in cornmeal-borax
Scotch broom	Air-dry upright. Tie to curved coat-hanger to change shape
Snapdragon	Horizontal, in silica gel, cornmeal-borax, reinforce stem with wire
Stock	Horizontal, in silica gel
Strawflower	Cut before fully open, air-dry hanging
Statice	Air-dry hanging
Sumac	Air-dry red fruits upright; press or iron leaves
Sunflower	Face down in sand or cornmeal-borax
Sweet-gum leaves	Cut before frost. Press or iron. Leaves keep color in glycerin (three days)
Sweet pea	Horizontal, in silica gel, cornmeal-borax
Tansy	Cut when blossoms mature, air-dry hanging
Violet	Press. Cure in sand, silica gel
Vinca minor	Submerge in glycerin solution
Vitex	Press foliage; dip seed stalks in thinned shellac
Winged Everlasting (Ammobium alatum)	Air-dry hanging
Yarrow	Air-dry hanging
Zinnia	Silica gel, cornmeal-borax, sand

VII
PERMANENT
FLOWERS OF
FEATHERS
WAX AND
SHELLS

Early explorers had returned from North America with amazing reports of a land where birds were numerous beyond belief. Though they had been forewarned, the settlers still were astounded to see the sun eclipsed by hundreds of thousands of passenger pigeons flying overhead. Wild ducks and wild geese, in migration, literally covered the surfaces of ponds and lakes. Huge flocks of pheasant, quail, and grouse rose up from tall grass with a thundering of wings; cardinals, orioles, tanagers, bluebirds and blue jays were lightning flashes of color against the sombre forest green. In the mockingbird, Virginia colonists even found an "American nightingale."

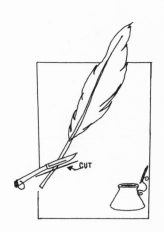

On the first Thanksgiving Day, turkey was the main dish at the feast; thus was established a two-fold tradition. The Pilgrims might have heard, before they left England, of these great wattled birds and their delicious meat—although the turkey was native only to the New World, it had been introduced in Spain in 1519 by explorers returning from Mexico. At any rate, English settlers promptly set about domesticating the turkey to take the place of the laying hens they so fondly remembered; wild ducks and geese could also be caught in snares and tamed. Wild pigeons grew plump and multiplied rapidly in captivity, so many a home boasted a dove cote that ensured a supply of succulent squab. Chickens, however, had to be imported, and they were scarce for many years.

Barnyard fowl were valued not only as meat for the table but as the best source of feathers for filling bedticks, pillows and bolsters and for making pens and dusters. The soft breast feathers of turkeys, ducks and geese went into ticks and bolsters, and Dutch colonists used them also in coverlets. Light, fluffy down was carefully saved for pillows. Long hard quills from the pinions of geese made the best pens, and as soon as paint became available, these wing feathers served as brushes. For dusters, color-hungry colonial housewives liked pheasant plumage interspersed with red and blue tail feathers from cardinals and jays. Turkey wings did double duty: they swept the ashes off the hearth, and swirled patterns on the sanded kitchen floor.

Peafowl, the most decorative of all domesticated birds, were imported early along with more useful but less ornamental poultry. Peacock tail feathers went into dusters, or were arranged in jugs on shelves or tables.

43. *In the study of the Audubon House in Key West, Florida, John James Audubon appropriately used a quill pen to write descriptions of the White-Crowned Pigeon and the Key-West Quail Dove. Other paintings made while he was a guest here in 1832 later appeared in print with the notation "Florida Keys" in their captions. In the collection at Audubon House is the complete original Double Elephant Folio Birds of America, finally at home in the house where Audubon did the sketches for many of its plates. The rare but ungainly bird perched on a piece of driftwood is a stuffed roseate spoonbill.*

Feather pictures were made quite early in the colonial period for wall *Colonial* decoration. Plucked plumage of pheasant and grouse (or songbirds) being *Feather Pictures* readied for the dinner table furnished the material, which was glued on paper or on thin strips of wood. Sometimes the feathers from several different species were combined to create an entirely fanciful, but always colorful, bird or animal. Brown- and white-speckled guinea feathers were welcomed as a contrast to solid color plumage; the small, smooth breast feathers, trimmed and overlapped, became the pelts of imaginary beasts.

Fluffy "flowers" could easily be made from pinfeathers, simply by *Early Feather Flowers* bunching and tying them together in a miniature version of the feather duster. It was an easy matter, too, to shape larger wing, neck, and tail feathers into petals with scissors, and to glue flat flower forms on cloth or paper. Flower pictures composed of feathers in their natural bright colors were very popular.

During the eighteenth century, chickens became common. Gradually, by crossing poultry strains from Asia and Europe, new American breeds were developed, among them an all-white variety called Plymouth Rock and the black-and-white Domernecker whose feathers looked like printed calico. Every nineteenth-century farm home had its hen house. In small towns, a few chickens usually were kept in a backyard pen. Even in large cities, poultry was bought live and dressed at home, so feathers were everywhere available. With all this raw material at hand, it would have been surprising if ingenious women had not found a way to use it in decorating.

Flowers made from the white feathers of ducks, geese, and Plymouth Rock hens and roosters were much admired in the second quarter of the nineteenth century. Because they were so easily cut with scissors, feathers could be made to resemble any petal or leaf. They could be steamed over a teakettle and curved or curled by pulling them through the fingers or over a dull knife blade.

Someone made the interesting discovery that chicken feathers could be dyed—this was not true of the plumage of ducks and geese, because of an oily coating that helped keep the birds afloat in water. It was possible, of course, to shape chicken feathers into a flower and dip the finished flower into dye, but the inner petals were apt to dry in streaks and blotches. A better method was to dye the feathers first, dry and fluff them in sun and wind, and then cut them with curved manicure scissors.

Flowers were formed by gluing feather petals individually to circles of paper or cardboard, beginning with the outside row and working toward the center. Then the blossoms, which often were surprisingly lifelike in accordance with the Victorian ideal of realism, were arranged in a wreath or a mound on a wooden base, and glued in place. Feather pictures of the colonial period, exposed to the drying effect of air and the ravages of insects, had gradually disintegrated to dust; knowing this, Victorian ladies placed their fragile wreaths and pyramids of feather flowers under bell-shaped glass domes. Thus protected, the flowers remained fresh and colorful for many years.

Dyed feathers were used in other ways. Tied together with matching thread around a stick-stem or glued as a unit to it, they formed flowers that could be arranged with iridescent peacock tail-feather foliage. Very often peacock feathers were used alone, in tall vases, and rivalled pampas grass as a parlor decoration. With glue (and patience) cut feathers could be combined on a background of dark velvet in facsimiles of birds or flowers; such pictures were placed in shadow-box frames beneath a sheet of glass.

Stuffed Birds   In the nineteenth century, amateurs dabbled in taxidermy. Country boys earned ready cash by trapping the still plentiful wild mink, beaver and raccoon; there was a ready market for the pelts, which were used not only by furriers but by hatters. To be salable, the skins had to be cured, and this was done by pegging out the stretched pelt, fur side down, on a board and drying it in the open air. When dry, the pelts were completely stiff, but they could be made pliable by rubbing the skin side with neat's foot oil.

Cooks had long known how to remove the plumage of a bird intact, by skinning—pheasants and turkeys often were roasted and returned to their skins for presentation•at the table, after the manner of the earlier dormants. Bird skins (with head, legs, and feet still attached) were prepared for mounting in the same way that pelts were cured. Once dried and oiled, they were sewed into shape over a firm stuffing of packed cotton. Tiny jet beads were glued into the eye sockets.

Once John James Audubon's paintings had made it fashionable to admire the whole bird and not the feathers only, stuffed birds became valued decorations for the home. The more colorful species were, of course, the most desirable; with a fine disregard for ornithology, a stuffed parrot from the tropical jungle of South America might share a perch with a Rocky Mountain bluebird. A "natural habitat" was created by affixing a short forked branch upright on a bed of dyed dry moss, and a domed glass cover was added to preserve the specimens from air, dust, and insects.

Making   The first Spanish explorers in Mexico found Indian chieftains wearing
Feather Flowers   plumed headdresses, and garments of dyed feathers sewn on cotton cloth. For his confrontation with Cortez, the great Montezuma was garbed in a marvelous feathered cloak, intricately patterned in jewel colors, that was part of the fabled treasure of the Aztecs.

Twentieth-century feather flowers are as colorful as Montezuma's cloak. They are sold by florists, specialty shops, and department stores, and ready-dyed materials for making them may be procured at hobby shops and (through a retail florist) from wholesale florists' suppliers. Airy maribou fluffs, one inch fluff tips, and three to six-inch fluffy feathers with square, smooth ends are all obtained from turkeys. Coque and hackle feathers, long and narrow, with rounded or pointed ends, once were the tail and neck plumage of roosters. Geese provide both naturally curved soft feathers and long, smooth stiff quills; pigeon quills are short, stiff, and narrow. All these forms may be bought in brilliant or pastel colors, but it is now possible to dye natural feathers—even those from ducks or geese. First they must be washed thoroughly *with detergent* (not soap) in warm water, to remove their coating of oil. Then they are immersed in a dye bath prepared in a quart-size glass jar, using liquid dye diluted with boiling water to which one tablespoonful of white vinegar has been added. A feather is held, with tongs or tweezers, by the tip of its shaft and swished back and forth in the liquid; it then is lifted and shaken to remove excess dye. Dyed feathers may be dried (tied in a cloth bag or an old pillow case) in an electric clothes dryer, at low heat, for fifteen minutes.

Steaming restores the fluffiness of home-dyed feathers, and makes commercially-colored feathers flexible and easy to curve. This is done by tying

them in small bunches and holding them just above the spout of a tea-kettle from which steam is escaping. While still limp, pull the dull edge of a table knife along the spine of a quill, repeating until the desired curve or curl is obtained. (Very stiff shafts that do not stay curled should be notched with a knife at quarter-inch intervals on the back side, and then steamed and stroked again.)

A most effective feather flower, and a very easy one to make, is the shasta daisy. Cut a disc one inch in diameter from heavy white paper or thin cardboard, and punch a small hole in its center. Select nine to twelve white pigeon quills similar in size, trimming their tips if necessary to make them all one to one-and-a-half inches in length. Cover one side of the disc with an even layer of white glue, using a flat toothpick as a spreader. Lay the feathers, face up, on the disc, so close together that their edges are overlapped at the base but are separated at the tip. Prepared "daisy peps" (centers) may be bought at hobby shops, but realistic centers can be made from yellow or orange ball fringe. Bend a two-foot length of all-purpose aluminum wire in the middle. Press the points through a fringe ball, pulling them down until the fuzzy ball hides the crook of the wire. Twist the two ends of wire together, beginning at the ball, and thread this twisted stem through the hole in the center of the paper daisy disc; a drop of glue on the back of the disc will steady the stem permanently. Wrap the twisted wires with green floral tape, inserting leaves at intervals during the wrapping process—these could be plastic daisy (or poppy) foliage, or green floral feathers separated and curled like paper ribbon over one blade of a pair of scissors.

Showy chrysanthemums and peonies of curled floral feathers are formed on small balls of white styrofoam. A stem of green florist's wire, bent to a miniature shepherd's crook at one end, is pulled through the ball until the tip of the crook is imbedded in the plastic foam. Approximately fifty feathers are required.

Begin with five short feathers, one and a half to two inches in length. Curl their tips by pulling them over a table knife or scissors blade. Dip the pointed shaft of each feather in white glue and press it into the top of the stemmed styrofoam ball; the curled tips should curve inward and overlap, so that the top of the ball is completely concealed. Curl nine slightly longer feathers for the second row of petals; glue and space them evenly around and over the first five. Make each row of petals a little fuller and a little longer than the one above it, and cover the entire ball. At least five rows will be needed to do so; the feathers in the fifth row should be four to four and a half inches long. For neatness, finish the underside of the chrysanthemum by slipping a green plastic calyx and cup over the wire stem, securing them against the base of the flower with a drop of glue.

In the late eighteenth century, wax profile portraits became so popular that special schools were established to teach the art to young ladies. In addition, these wax-work schools taught their pupils to carve and model wax in fruit and flower forms. The basis of the craft was beeswax, used alone or in combination with spermaceti (a white wax substance obtained from the heads of sperm whales) to lighten its color and lessen crumbling.

In making profile portraits, melted wax was poured into small shallow tin pan-molds that were round, oval, or rectangular in shape; the wax

COLONIAL WAX PORTRAITS

shrank as it cooled, and when the thin slab had completely hardened, it lay loose in the mold. On such a medallion, a profile likeness of Washington, Lafayette, or some other Revolutionary War hero was carved, like a cameo, in relief. Outlining could be done with a wooden-handled shoemaker's awl; the point was heated in a candle flame for ease of etching and to keep the wax from breaking under pressure. A heated penknife blade was used to shear away the background. Fine lines were drawn, and detailed carving done, with a common pin warmed between the fingers.

Hundreds of such portrait medallions were made but only a few still exist, for although wax was easy to work with, it was extremely fragile. The creamy color of wax showed up well against a dark background, so the medallions often were mounted on black velvet in shadow-box frames. Even under glass, the color of the wax gradually darkened with age to tan, and then to ochre-brown.

Molded Wax   About the time that kerosene was replacing whale oil as the fuel for lamps, a new kind of mineral wax called paraffin began to be produced as a by-product of the petroleum industry. Paraffin was cheaper and more stable than beeswax or spermaceti; consequently, wax-work was revived in the late 1840's and achieved instant success in England and the United States. At the Great Exhibition of 1851 in London's Crystal Palace, an entire section was devoted to the display of wax flowers; modelling in wax was proclaimed not merely a craft but an important art form. Directions for modelling fruits and flowers were printed in periodicals, and newspaper advertisements offered two-part molds for making wax fruits, flowers, animals and birds—ladies unskilled in sculpture hastened to buy them. Some such molds were composed of two hollowed sections that screwed together, one on top of the other; the melted wax was poured in through a small hole at the top. When the wax had set, it was a simple matter to dip the mold in hot water, unscrew and lift off the top section, and remove the wax apple or rose. A small seam might show where the two halves of the mold had joined, but this could easily be smoothed away with a heated knife blade.

Wax fruits usually were arranged in plaster of Paris baskets; both basket molds and ready-made plastic baskets could be bought. The favorite wax flowers for filling baskets, arranging in vases, or making into wreaths were orange blossoms, lilies, and fuchsias. Usually the flowers and fruits were painted after they were modelled or molded, but occasionally a drop or two of artist's oil paint was worked into softened wax to color it in advance. When the composition was complete, it was placed under a glass dome for protection and was proudly displayed on a mantel or a parlor table.

Waxed Flowers   Realism was the watchword of Victorian craftsmen, and soon someone suggested coating fresh, live flowers with wax. The idea was eagerly seized upon; not everyone could model (or even mold) flowers successfully, but anyone could (and did) dip a blossom into a kettle of melted wax. For this sentimental era, there was a further advantage: waxed bridal bouquets and funeral wreaths could be preserved under glass domes as lasting home decorations and reminders.

44. *This close-up of a wax flower arrangement at the Tallman House in Janesville, Wisconsin, shows how the serrated foliage and trailing lines preferred for Victorian fresh flower arrangements were carried over into more permanent decorations made of wax. The dipped blossoms have retained their shape perfectly, although their colors are somewhat faded after more than a century under glass. All the "flowers of romance" are here: roses, orange blossoms, freesias, fuchsias, lilies of the valley, and sweet peas. Narcissi, daisies and carnations lend a touch of everyday cheerfulness, while trailing ivy adds a somber note.*

Exposed to the air, wax-coated blossoms gradually lose their color. The process, however, is simple, and the product a conversation piece. Obviously the natural colors of the blossoms are dimmed by their coating of semiopaque wax, but white petals become whiter and attain a pearly luminescence. This explains the prevalence of Bermuda and calla lilies, lilies of the valley, orange blossoms, white roses and white sweet peas in Victorian waxed flower bouquets. In selecting colored blooms for waxing, choose deep, bright hues. These will be lightened to pastels by the waxing process: bright red emerges deep pink; orange alters to apricot; gold lightens to yellow; purple becomes lavender, and sometimes changes to blue or rose.

In a deep saucepan, over low heat, melt four half-pound blocks of paraffin (from drugstore or supermarket) with two ounces of spermaceti (which a druggist can order) and one inch of a large white wax candle. Use a candy thermometer to determine when the wax reaches a temperature of 130°; turn off the heat. Hold a blossom by its stem and dip it into the melted wax, which should be deep enough to cover the entire flower head; lift it out immediately and shake it over the pan to remove excess wax. Separate the petals, if necessary, with the tip of a paring knife. Stand the flower upright in a soft drink bottle to dry. After about ten minutes, hold the flower right side up over the pan, and spoon the reheated wax over its stem and leaves. It the wax coating is not perfect, the flower may be redipped. Return the flower to its bottle and leave it undisturbed overnight before arranging; use a separate bottle for drying each dipped flower so that petals and leaves will not be crowded. Lilies of the valley, sweet peas, orange blossoms, fuchsias, and (surprisingly) full-blown roses take kindly to this method of preservation; heavy, many-petalled blooms, such as chrysanthemums and zinnias, do not.

SHELLS Since shells were plentiful and beautiful, and a gift from the sea, gathering them for decorative use was a pleasant pastime for women and children in colonial days. Large perfect specimens were arranged in a row on a shelf, heaped in a basket on a window sill or table, or used as pin trays and flower containers. Seashells were practical as well as pretty. Then as now, scallop shells served as individual baking dishes. Large flat clamshells were used to skim the fat from soups or the cream from milk. Early settlers in Boston ate their cornmeal mush with clamshell spoons; a small shell formed the bowl and a cleft stick the handle.

Wampum, the common medium of exchange within and among the various Indian tribes, consisted of cylindrical fragments of quahaug, whelk, and periwinkle shells, rubbed smooth on stones and strung like beads on leather thongs. Purple beads, from quahaug shells, had twice the value of white whelk and periwinkle wampum. Indians displayed their wealth, like jewelry, in personal adornments. Strings of wampum beads, arranged in patterns by color, were worn as necklaces or woven together into belts and headbands.

Colonial
Shell Composition Colonial women soon noticed that some of the tiniest shells were especially colorful and pleasing of form; they began to glue small shells to paper or to wood in patterns that resembled mosaics.

It was easy to see that cup, clam, and jingle shells had the shape of rounded flower petals. Bonefish scales were fluted like the petals of carnations. Garfish scales were irregularly shaped and pointed, like leaves. Teardrop shells resembled the slender petals of a daisy or a zinnia; baby conch and small snail shells looked like flower buds, elongated or flat. Once the similarity of shape was recognized, the next step was to glue the shells together into flower forms. In early days, these were made directly on thin wood panels, as part of an overall design that might also include bird, animal and human figures modelled of wax, cardboard houses, and trees made from cotton against a background shell mosaic.

In the nineteenth century, shell work reached the zenith of its popularity in tall massed pyramids of shell flowers for mantels, niches, and tables. At first the materials for these had to be gathered at the seashore, but by mid-century shells could be purchased in sets, with patterns for various flower forms and instructions for making them. Victorian shell flowers were made on circles of cardboard or stiff paper, and mounded flowers were built around tufts of cotton; the shells were often painted for greater versimilitude. Completed flowers were attached with dabs of plaster to a plaster cone or glued to a wooden form, touching and overlapping in a tight grouping that entirely concealed the base. Roses were not difficult to make, and were almost invariably a part of such a composition, but smaller garden flowers and fruit-tree blossoms were necessary fillers, and shell leaves were used as accents. For trailing over the lip and down the side of the container, minuscule teardrop or coquina shells were glued together into florets of wistaria or fuchsia, and the florets in turn were glued to stems of wire or straw.

Victorian Shell Craft

Often a shell pyramid topped an elaborate ornamental vase, with hand-painted decorations that repeated the colors and forms of the shell flowers. Sometimes the container was of molded plaster, decorated with still more shell flowers. A protective glass dome that might be two and a half to three feet tall covered pyramid and container; usually these arrangements were made in pairs, for use at either end of a mantel or a piano.

Not all Victorian shell flowers were arranged in urns or vases, for shell pictures were much admired. In making these, a thin sheet of wood or heavy cardboard was covered with black or deep-blue velvet; shell flowers and leaves, with stems of dyed straw, were glued to the material—sometimes in a bouquet tied with velvet ribbon, sometimes as an arrangement that brimmed from a container made of a large flat scallop shell. Shadow-box frames were necessary for these three-dimensional pictures, or a convex glass covering to keep them free of dust.

In the 1890's, a shell-trimmed trinket box stood on every parlor whatnot. The vast majority of these were made of cardboard coated with plaster of Paris; shells pressed into the plaster while it was wet were immovably attached once the surface dried. It was the fashion first to cover the entire box with an encrustation of tiny shells and then to add, with dabs of extra plaster, a further ornamentation of painted shell flowers.

See-through portieres were the turn-of-the-century equivalent of latter day room dividers. These were made of many strands of beads or shells,

45.   *In the drawing room of Fountain Elms, built in 1850 in Utica, New York, arched niches with curved backs provide the ideal setting for a pair of unusually fine shell flower arrangements. Here the characteristic plaster urn is encrusted with tiny shells in an effect not unlike hobnail glass. Large and small shells have been artfully glued together into many recognizable flower species, among them zinnias, calendulas, primroses, dahlias, daisies, and the inevitable Victorian roses. The glass dome fits close around and over the composition; the total height of the decoration is thirty-five and one half inches.*

46. *This sea-shell castle scene from the Stenton Mansion in Philadelphia was made by Anna Reckless Emlen in 1757. Against a background mosaic of small dark shells embellished with shell roses, the white building stands out clearly on its cliff of larger shells resembling boulders. The steps are of cardboard; the stick picket fence has a shell railing. The trees are tufts of green-dyed cotton, and the human figures wear cotton cloth. Among the wax creatures at the base of the cliff are three passenger pigeons (now an extinct species).*

tied at the top to a brass rod but loose and swinging free at the bottom. Polished olive shells were preferred for portieres; they were bored at each end and threaded lengthwise on twisted cord strong enough to support their considerable combined weight. As many as twelve hundred strung shells were required to curtain a doorway.

In the days before the invention of the indispensible zipper, rows of white "pearl" buttons trimmed and closed baby dresses, children's clothes, men's shirts, and ladies' summer gowns; they ranged in size from one-eighth inch to two inches in diameter. These were stamp-cut from the thick layer of nacre that lined the inner surface of fresh water mussel shells. Bits of this same pearly white material, as well as pieces of the darkly iridescent lining of abalone shells from Mexico and California, were extensively used as inlays to embellish boxes, lap-desks, and tables—useful as well as decorative inlaid tables were topped with chessboards of alternate squares of white and dark mother-of-pearl. Some inlay work was done at home, to ornament wooden box-tops. Thin sheets of mother-of-pearl could be bought from jewelers; soaked in warm water, these became pliable and could be cut with shears or with a sharp knife but there was considerable waste because the nacre often split. A design of a flower or a geometric motif was traced on the box lid and reamed out lightly with a tiny chisel and a tack hammer. Fish glue was used to attach the fitted slivers of mother-of-pearl.

Each successive generation has felt the fascination of shell collecting, and Americans have always liked to put their finds to use. Making shell flowers is, however, a hobby that need not be pursued only at the seashore. From hobby shops and mail order catalogues, many varieties of shells of diverse shapes and sizes may be bought in their natural wide range of colors. Also available are clear plastic discs from one-half inch to two inches in diameter, findings for costume jewelry, plastic foliage, and plastic-coated wire stems, as well as special shell glue and waterproof finishing lacquer.

Shells gathered along the beach must be cleaned thoroughly, by washing them with a brush in warm soapsuds and rinsing in clear water, and their appearance often is improved by bleaching. This is done by soaking them in a cup of warm water to which a tablespoonful of liquid household chlorine bleach has been added. The required soaking time varies with the size and thickness of the shells; half a minute may suffice for tiny seed conch, while large convoluted shells will require half an hour or more. After a thorough rinsing and a re-washing with soap and water, their surfaces may be made more lustrous by rubbing with two parts mineral oil thinned with one part lighter fluid. Although shells sold in shops are clean and odor-free, they often benefit by bleaching and polishing with oil.

Directions for
Shell Flowers

47. *This shell wreath, now at the Thomas Cooke House in Edgarton, Massachusetts, was made in 1870 by Mrs. Mary A. Edson. It affords a close-up view of the extreme precision and delicacy of the best Victorian shellwork. The smaller flowers in the center are in a glass-covered circular shadow box; its wide frame is completely covered with shells of various sizes, and twelve shell roses have been added at intervals that correspond to the numerals on a clock. Perhaps the arrangement symbolized the slow passage of time—Mrs. Edson is thought to have whiled away a long winter at this craftwork while waiting for her husband's return from a whaling voyage.*

One of the most interesting aspects of shell-flower making is the selection and matching of shells for natural color and shading. However, to provide a special effect or to reinforce a natural hue, diluted hot liquid glue may be applied with a small artist's brush; artificially colored shells must be very thoroughly coated with lacquer to make them waterproof and to prevent fading. Fish scales for leaves or petals may be colored by immersing them in cool, diluted dye; they should then be rinsed and dried between paper towels, under weight. They also must be brushed or sprayed with lacquer to seal in the dye.

No hard and fast rule requires that a specific shell be used to make a particular flower form, but certain common shells are generally employed for the following purposes:

Buds: whole olive, snail, small conch, cerith, and young whelk shells, or a matched pair of "butterfly" coquinas glued face to face around a pledget of cotton.
Florets: coquina, tiny rose cups or minature white cups, baby snail, or barnacles.
Round petals: cup, rose cup, lucina, elegant docinia, cockle, translucent jingle, fluted scallop.
Ovoid petals: tampa tellin, egg cockle, coquina.
Irregularly shaped petals: kitten's paws, bonefish and garfish scales.
Slender petals: Job's tears, rice shells.
Centers: tiny ceriths and rice shells, snail or olive shell tops, sea-urchin skeletons, cup-and-saucer limpets, yellow-dyed lilac shells, coral "buttons" (plus mustard and poppy seeds, peppercorns, and whole allspice).
Stamens: thread-coral, tube-shaped dentalions (tooth shells), seaweed stems well coated with lacquer as a preservative.

An especially lovely flower is the open tea rose made of apricot-pink jingle shells on a three-quarter-inch plastic disc bored with two holes to receive a stem. Thread the ends of a twelve-inch length of green plastic wire through the two holes; pull one end down, leaving the other end an inch and a half long. Twist the short end twice around the longer stem to hold the disc level and steady. Mask the twisted portion of the stem with green floral tape. Cover the top of the disc, including the flat loop of wire, evenly with shell glue or clear household cement, using a flat toothpick as a spreader. Lay over this a thin layer of wisps of absorbent cotton dipped in glue. Place a circle of five one-inch jingle shells face up on the cotton with their hinges toward the stem—these should overlap slightly near the rim of the disc, to hide the plastic. Add a layer of glue-dipped cotton to the center of the disc, allowing it to extend over the shallow hinges of the lower row of petals. Fit the hinges of a second circle of smaller jingle shells into the hollows of the first row, and tilt the shells upward at a 30° angle. Around a third, mounded layer of glue-dipped cotton, balance a third row of still smaller petals at a 60° angle. Finally, fit three small jingle shells upright around a minute ball of glue-soaked cotton in the middle of the rose, tipping them inward until their upper edges touch to form the flower's center. After the glue has set, brush (or spray) the rose with shell lacquer.

Full-blown roses also are made, by the same method, of lucina, elegant docinia, and cup shells. Small fruit-tree blossoms, which have only five petals, are simulated with rose or white cup shells on a half-inch disc, with a pointed baby Whelk or a round yellow mustard seed for a center. These are more realistic when their discs are cemented to an actual twig or branch.

COTTON

Composite flower heads, such as lilac, hydrangea, or geranium, are clusters of individual blossoms too small to be made on discs; such tiny flowers are constructed directly on the tops of short wires that are then bunched and wrapped together into an umbel. In a bridal wreath (*Spiraea vanhouttei*) cluster, each floret has five petals, and each slightly mounded head contains several of the infinitesimal flowers. A spray of spirea is therefore troublesome to make, but is a tremendously effective addition to an arrangement of mixed shell flowers.

Cut green bell-wire (or very fine green-coated florist's wire) in four-inch lengths. Coil one end of each short wire into a circle one-fourth inch in diameter; bend and adjust each coil so that it is flat at right angles to the stem. Cover the coil with wisps of cotton dredged in glue. Select five white cup shells no more than one-fourth inch across; with tweezers, arrange them in a circle, face up, on the cotton and add one yellow mustard seed for a center. Stand the finished floret upright in a shot glass to dry while others are being made. After the glue has set, coat both top and bottom of each floret with shell lacquer. Gather five or six florets into a cluster, bending their stems to do so, and allow their petals to overlap a little. Bind the flexible wires together with green floral tape, and then bend the bound stalk at right angles, one inch from its end. With a second length of floral tape, secure the cluster to a long green plastic stem. Add other composite flower heads and small green serrated plastic leaves to complete the spray.

Since the shell flowers have been lacquered, and their stems and foliage are of plastic, they will be washable in soap or mild detergent and warm water. Flowers similarly made on discs, but without stems, are used in costume jewelry by cementing the disc to pin- or earring-backs.

VIII
EARLY
PAPER
CRAFTS

In the seventeenth century, paper was classed as a luxury and used with restraint. Aside from oiled paper, which was a substitute for window glass, the busy colonists used paper only for writing purposes, and they had precious little time for writing. A copybook, homemade of pages sewed together at the fold, was the cherished possession of eighteenth-century schoolboys. Even in the nineteenth century, paper was too scarce to be wasted on children just learning to write—they graduated to ruled tablet paper only after much practice on a slate.

Paper, invented in China but named for the Egyptian papyrus, did not come into general European use until the fifteenth century—just in time to make the printing press a practical invention. In Asia, it had been made of the bark of the paper-mulberry tree, but Europeans used cotton or linen rags, boiled and ground to a pulp, rolled out and spread to dry in thin layers between sheets of felt. Rag paper was used exclusively in America until the mid-nineteenth century. This paper was thicker than the machine-rolled pine pulp product that supplanted it, and far more durable. By comparison, it yellowed very little, and did not dry out or crumble quickly; for this reason, many manuscripts and some examples of paper craftwork have come down intact to the present day.

SILHOUETTES   In eighteenth-century America, the *shadowgraph* was a novel innovation. In this primitive forerunner of photography, the subject to be "limned" sat sideways before a candle, so that the shadow of his (or her) profile was cast upon a sheet of paper tacked to the wall. By carefully drawing around the shadow, a likeness was produced; compared with the work of the average itinerant portrait painter of the period, such a profile was startlingly realistic and discouragingly unflattering. For contrast, these shadow outlines were tinted, or filled in with black ink.

Artists were able to dispense with the cast shadow, drawing much smaller profile portraits freehand and inking them in. These were of a size suitable for framing, and became an acceptable substitute for more expensive painted miniatures. In France, in 1759, these economical shadow miniatures were derisively christened *silhouettes*, after Etienne de Silhouette, Minister of Finance under Louis XV, who was despised for his personal penury and detested for his indifference to the plight of the poor. As a result of this jest, his surname came into international usage as the name of the black-on-white profile portrait.

In Europe, especially in Germany and Switzerland, *scheren-schnitten* was already popular; it was the art of cutting designs from paper with small, sharp scissors. Before long, European and American artists were

48. *This delightful group portrait, made about 1844, depicts the Jelleff family of Newark, New Jersey. The figures represent John Jelleff's Quaker mother, his wife, their three daughters, and the* pater familias *himself. The cutter's name does not appear on the face of the framed and glazed scene, but the style is strongly reminiscent of the work of the French silhouettist Augustin Edouart who toured the United States between 1839 and 1849. Edouart was famous for group silhouettes, and had a flair for appropriate backgrounds. The label he attached to the back of some of his cuttings read in part:*

> *Mons. Edouart . . . begs to observe that his Likenesses are produced by the scissors alone, and are preferable to any taken by machines . . . in a style which has not hitherto been attempted by any other artist.*

The large silhouette, twenty by twenty-three and a half inches, is in the collection of the Newark Museum.

applying this technique to silhouettes, cutting the profile outline from black paper and pasting it on white. Americans were not long content to leave the scissors in the hands of professionals. Young ladies in particular were eager to test their skill. Nelly Custis, for example, whiled away several evenings at Mount Vernon, cutting profiles of her grandparents George and Martha Washington, trying to catch a likeness by observing their shadows on the wall.

There was a second type of scissored picture in which the profile was first outlined on white paper; then all the area within the outline was carefully trimmed away, leaving a hollow-cut silhouette. The whole sheet of white paper, with the cut out at its center, was placed over black silk.

Silhouettists began to tour the states, taking likenesses by one method or the other. A small portable "machine" had been invented that automatically reduced an actual shadow to a much smaller outline for hollow-cuts, and many professionals used one. Charles Wilson Peale and William Bache were famous hollow-cutters, but William Henry Brown stuck to scissors—it was his boast that he could cut a detailed likeness in one minute. Entire figures obviously were harder to cut than heads alone, so full-length silhouettes were particularly admired. These often were mounted on a background prepared in advance: a lithograph, showing a landscape with trees, a room with views beyond the windows, or a formal garden.

Portraits of famous men, cut by well-known silhouettists, were reproduced for sale; Washington's profile, in black on white, was indelibly stamped upon the pages of history. Less familiar after two hundred years are other forms of paper craft that also were highly esteemed in colonial days.

CUTOUT PATTERNS

At the time of the American Revolution, the ability to cut ornamental patterns from stiff paper was deemed a useful accomplishment for young ladies. Every school child has heard that Betsy Ross created a five-pointed star for the first American flag with one snip of her scissors, but few girls (or their mothers) could now duplicate the feat. Almost the sole survival of this craft is the string of paper dolls. A long strip of paper, folded many times accordion style, is cut in the shape of half a figure and unfolded; behold, a whole row of paper dolls in wide skirts and bonnets, holding hands.

PAPYROTAMIA

Although the high-sounding name *papyrotamia* was applied to all cut-paper art, it came to mean specifically an intricate scene cut from stiff white paper. Most of this work was done by ladies with artistic ability, free time, sharp scissors, and very steady hands. First they pinned a large sheet of heavy paper to a board, and drew upon it a freehand design in in pencil. Large blank areas were excised with the sharpened tip of a pen-knife. Then the paper was removed from the board, and the difficult task of trimming was done with scissors especially made for this purpose in Germany. Their long, thin, pointed blades, shaped like the bill of a stork, were honed razor sharp. Landscapes, complete with recognizable animals and birds, street scenes replete with an amazing wealth of detail, bouquets of mixed flowers and baskets of mixed fruits were achieved by this method, to the astonishment of persons less gifted or less patient. The best pieces of papyrotamia were mounted on black paper, framed, and glazed; often they were bequeathed to a favorite relative or friend.

PIERCED PAPER

Only slightly less effective were pierced paper designs, made with pins of various sizes. Originally these had served as stencils for transferring embroidery patterns, but by the mid-eighteenth century they had become unbelievably complex and an end in themselves. They were difficult to make, because the design could be traced on the paper only in the form of dots so small that they would disappear when pricked with a pin. The paper

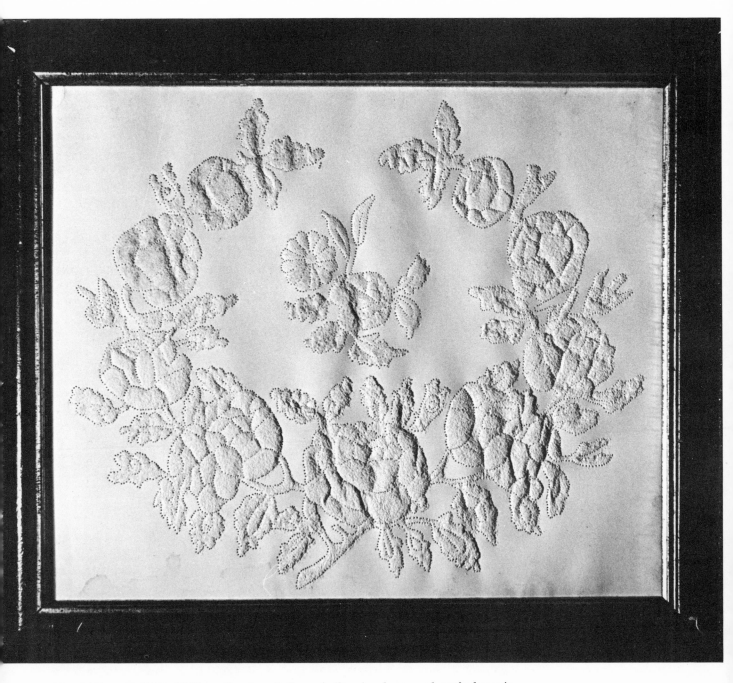

49. *In the mid-1850's, William Morrison Tallman built a handsome and costly home in Janesville, Wisconsin. Mr. Tallman was well known as an abolitionist, and his new house was rumored to be a station on the "underground railway," by which fleeing slaves were helped to reach the safety of the Canadian border. In the collection of the Rock County Historical Society, displayed at Tallman House, is this framed, pricked-paper floral wreath. The design was made by piercing the paper with pins of various sizes, which created a raised effect. When pricked-paper designs were painted with water colors, they closely resembled padded stumpwork cloth pictures of the eighteenth century.*

was laid flat on a board, and the holes were made with pins or needles run through small blocks of cork to protect the fingers. Favorite designs were wreaths, closely followed by baskets of flowers; these were mounted over black paper or cloth, and framed for hanging.

A variant of this technique was the *repoussé* design. After a picture had been created by pricking, certain portions of the design were raised; this was done by wetting the back of the paper and stretching it very carefully with the slightly rounded tip of a teaspoon. Once the paper had dried, the back was stiffened with sizing (thinned glue) to preserve the padded look. In the first half of the nineteenth century, when this craft was at the height of its popularity, it was customary to paint the raised motifs with watercolors and the effect was very similar to that of eighteenth-century stumpwork done on cloth.

EMBROIDERY
ON PAPER

In the nineteenth–century needlepoint, under the name Berlin Work, became the most fashionable type of embroidery. The canvas on which the designs were worked in colored worsted was quite costly, and many needlewomen found a substitute for it in perforated cardboard or paper. When these fragile materials were stitched over with silk floss or fine woolen thread, they were made more durable. Berlin Work on cardboard could be fashioned into bookmarks and cardcases; the more delicate perforated paper was reserved for framed mottoes and small pictures.

PAPER LACE

Paper lace was a variant of the scenic papyrotamia. It also was made of stiff paper and cut with scissors, but the design was composed of repeated motifs separated by "bridges" no larger than a thread; sometimes the pattern of an actual piece of thread lace was traced on paper for cutting. When paper lace was used for Valentines, it often was made in the shape of a heart. Infinitesimal rosebuds, lover's knots, entwined hearts, and winged cupids covered the surface. Although most paper lace was white, it was occasionally made of gilded or silvered paper—as a matter of fact, present-day lacy mats and doilies are very similar to (and no more intricate than) their eighteenth- and nineteenth-century models that were painstakingly cut by hand.

COATS OF ARMS

Another specialized application of the craft of *scheren-schnitten* was the coat of arms. The design was traced with white ink or pointed chalk on black paper, cut out with scissors, and mounted on a diamond shape of white paper or white silk. In this stark form, the coat of arms became a hatchment; it usually was made as a memorial to a deceased family member.

MONTAGE

All these manifestations of papyrotamia combined black and white. Only rarely did colored paper figure in such designs, for the very good reason that colored paper itself was rare. Occasionally a *montage* was made in color; small animal, bird, or fruit motifs cut from hand-tinted papers were

50. *Woodlawn Plantation, a gift from George Washington to his ward, and now the property of the National Trust for Historic Preservation, has many treasured heirlooms from Mount Vernon, along with drawings and needlework of rare charm made by Nelly Custis Lewis herself. In 1850, then widowed and bereft of her children, she made this needle-picture as a "momento of sincere affection" for a friend. The design of a cabbage rose with buds and leaves was traced on perforated paper and worked in silk; within its frame, the embroidery is edged with a stamped gold border.*

51. *Lacy eighteenth-century Valentines were cut freehand with scissors from strong white rag paper. Doves, hearts, and flowers were favorite motifs, and the larger segments of a design were joined by thread-like "bridges." This example of early American paper lace is from the collection of the Cooper-Hewitt Museum of Design, Smithsonian Institution, in New York City.*

combined and mounted on a white or black background. Montages were sometimes landscapes, too. For one of these, a background of green hills and mountains shading from the purple to pale blue was considered a must, and it was thought proper to add pencil shading to the completed picture.

In 1774, a type of montage that harked back to the craft of freehand *scheren-schnitten* was originated by Mary Granville Delany, a witty English lady of fashion. Mrs. Delany, who was then seventy-four years of age, had long since distinguished herself as an artist working in oil, crayon, pastel, and pen-and-ink; she also was an avid student of botany. By idle experimentation, she discovered that it was possible to cut petals, stems, leaves and stamens of various flowers freehand from Chinese, French and English "stained papers" and to assemble the components by pasting them on black-washed Chinese paper. She called her compositions "paper mosaics." On her eighty-fifth birthday she retired from mosaic making, but by this time she had completed one thousand flower pictures, using live plants mounted on black paper as models. Mrs. Delany's *Flora* were botanically accurate and triumphantly artistic. With the exception of ten that were bequeathed to Queen Charlotte, her flower mosaics (preserved in ten large calf-bound ledgers) are in the possession of the British Museum.

Mrs. Delany's Paper Mosaics

Inspired by Mrs. Delany's achievements, a brief fad for flower montages swept England and the United States. Baskets, their weaving indicated by careful slitting with a knife point, showed up extremely well, and were the most popular containers for blossoms whose petals, stems, and leaves were cut out individually, with curved-bladed scissors, and added piece by piece to the composition. Lacy ferns, or leaves with serrated edges, often trailed from the sides of the basket.

In France and England, men as well as women found cutting-out and pasting-up a fascinating and creative hobby. In the years between 1811 and 1814, the great romantic poet, Lord Byron, worked on a famous four-fold screen, decorating one side with portraits of his favorite theatrical personages cut from prints and engravings in contemporary books, and covering the other side with action portraits of pugilists plus programs and tickets from boxing matches. The result was lively and witty, and highly individualistic—the same effect sought by twentieth-century practitioners of the art of montage.

Lord Byron's Screen

In eighteenth-century England, every lady had a "compendium." This was not, as might be supposed, an abridged dictionary, but a wooden box in which vials of medicine and boxes of cosmetics were collected and neatly stored. It was not unlike the make-up box on a twentieth-century dressing table.

ENGLISH PAPER FILIGREE QUILLWORK

Often the top of a compendium would be given a raised edge, like a gallery tray, and within this frame a decorative design was applied in *paper filigree*. Although the name suggests papyrotamia, this was a unique craft. Paper was cut, not in designs, but in strips approximately one-fourth of an inch wide. These strips, in turn, were cut into pieces about an inch long. Each bit of paper was lightly dampened and rolled over the smooth shaft of a feather, and its overlapping ends were carefully glued together. Placed on end and glued side by side to the compendium top, these tiny cylinders resembled a honeycomb; when their upper edges were delicately painted or gilded, the honeycomb took on the look of a mosaic.

The narrow strips were not always cut short and rolled into tubes. Sometimes they were left long, and only their dampened ends were coiled around the quill. When one such strip was balanced on edge, it resembled the curled frond of an unfolding fern. Several, of graduated length, placed side by side and turned in one direction, looked rather like a spray of lily of the valley. If the graduated strips were alternately faced left and right, the look was that of an ostrich plume.

When the craze for paper filigree reached the colonies, the craft was called *quillwork,* because the shaft of a feather was used to curl the paper strips. Confusion resulted, for this name already was applied to an entirely different and indigenous craft.

INDIAN QUILLWORK

Many Indian tribes used porcupine quills for decorating leather. The quills were dyed in bright colors, cut in even lengths, and arranged in patterns—the sunburst was a favorite and very attractive design—or applied in contiguous ladders that covered the surface of, say, a leather bib.

The colonists adopted porcupine quillwork, using it as the Indians often did on soft deerskin. Indian moccasins were infinitely more comfortable than European shoes of the colonial period, and easier to make—neither shoes nor moccasins were shaped to right or left foot. The settlers began by making and trimming moccasins for the tender feet of babies and small children. Pride prevented adults from wearing such footgear in public (at least in the cities) so moccasins were used as house-slippers. Porcupine quills and bright glass beads were sewn on, in Indian designs or in flower patterns.

AMERICAN PAPER QUILLWORK

In the Boston *Gazette* for May 26, 1775, the following advertisement appeared:

> This is to give notice, That Mrs. Hiller still continues to Keep School in Hanover Street . . . where young Ladies may be taught Wax Work, Transparent and Filligree, painting on Glass, Quill work and Feather work, Japanning, Embroidering with Silver and Gold, Tentstitch . . .

Since both "Filligree" and "Quill work" are mentioned, it is possible that the knowledgeable Mrs. Hiller gave instruction in both crafts. It is certain that the type of paper-filigree work she taught to her young ladies was very different from that originally practiced in England.

In the colonies, paper quillwork was customarily applied not to the tops of compendiums but to wooden plaques that might be framed in shadow boxes but more often served as back-plates for wall candle sconces. In this transformation, quillwork ceased to be merely paper work, and became three-dimensional *collage*—it could, in fact, be termed eighteenth-century pop-art.

Small sections of the design usually were in honeycomb mosaic, and a border of curled paper foliage was often included, but the remaining surface of the plaque was given over to other materials. Any small decorative object might be used—if it were bright-colored or shiny, so much the better. Shells, seeds, pebbles, bits of mica or mother-of-pearl, cones, burrs, cotton pods, dried flowers, straw, diminutive wax figurines and spirals of

52. *For decades, Salem, Massachusetts, was the seaport center of the Yankee shipping trade. The captains of her clipper ships built impressive houses and filled them with beautiful furniture, paintings and china from Europe and the Orient. Their wives and daughters occupied their time while waiting for the return of the ships with such ladylike pursuits as quillwork, called paper filigree in England, where the craft originated. This example from Essex Institute in Salem was made by Mary Jennison in 1770. Around the top and sides of the arched panel is a succession of flower forms made of narrow strips of paper glued on edge. Shells are used with restraint. Wire outlines the container in the center.*

silver or copper wire were all eligible to be combined with the paper in an effect that was busy but surprisingly harmonious.

Each element of the design was glued separately to the wood backing. Placing relatively large dried flowers and cones was child's play in comparison to working with quilled paper. A steady hand and a sure eye were required to set a minute cylinder on end or a curled scroll on edge; such painstaking work has since been much admired, but was only briefly emulated.

PASTED WALLPAPER

In the eighteenth century, handpainted wallpaper was brought from China in the East India Company's ships, but it was so expensive that few colonists could afford it. French and English wallpapers were imported as early as 1712; they, too, were beyond the price the average citizen could pay. Before imported paper was hung, the wall was given a basic covering of cloth, which was glued to the plaster and allowed to dry thoroughly. This provided a backing to which the paper clung when pasted. So good was the quality of Chinese and French papers, and so satisfactory was the method of hanging, that some papered walls are in perfect condition after two hundred years.

The first American wallpapers, made in Philadelphia in 1739, were reproductions of French and Chinese designs, and similar patterns are available today. Documentary wallpapers offered by such firms as Schumacher, Brunschwig & Fils, Katzenbach & Warren, and Strahan are copies of papers actually found on the walls of eighteenth- and nineteenth-century houses.

Wallpaper-Covered Boxes

Since both the imported and domestic varieties of vintage wallpaper were expensive, they were hung with extreme care to avoid waste. When trimming was absolutely necessary, every scrap of the paper, no matter how small, was collected and saved. The larger pieces, applied with cornstarch paste, were used to cover hatboxes and bandboxes, and to line domed travelling trunks. Small, irregularly shaped bits were pieced together to cover or line trinket boxes.

HAND-BLOCKED PAPERS

Very late in the eighteenth century, as an economy measure, wallpaper borders were sometimes used as a finishing touch on painted walls; wide borders for papered *and* painted walls became fashionable in the early 1800's. Very few women had attempted to make their own wallpaper, but these long strips of hand-blocked paper looked easier to do; ingenious (or impecunious) ladies were not slow to copy borders that were commercially produced.

The technique was the same as for printing cloth: carved wooden blocks were used—a separate block for each color of the design—with ink or dye. Most blocks were small, only about an inch thick, and sometimes no more than an inch across. Printed paper patterns differed from those on cloth in that they were more closely spaced. The block was inked and pressed down on the stretched paper, re-inked and set down so close to the first impression that it barely touched, and this process was continued until the entire surface had been covered. For greater decorative value, several colors were almost invariably employed. This meant that the whole process was repeated several times, each time with a different block, to overset the basic design with the desired colors. All this required considerable neatness

53. *Even among the 110 magnificent rooms of the Winterthur Museum, the Chinese Parlor is outstanding. The Parlor is dominated by its wallpaper, painted in China about 1770. Scenes of Chinese life in bright, clear colors have remained fresh and unfaded, and form an exotic background for beautiful Chippendale furniture and black-and-gold lacquer screens.*

and much patience, so ladies who practiced the craft were content to make their hand-blocked paper in small quantities. As a matter of fact, since it was used primarily to cover small boxes, a little of it went a long way.

In the eighteenth century, oriental lacquer work was as highly esteemed in France as in England, but whereas British ladies strove to capture its effect with stencils and paint, the ladies of France followed a different imitative technique. A trimmed print, or a motif cut from hand-painted Chinese or French wallpaper, was glued to the surface of a painted tray.

DECOUPAGE IN
THE EIGHTEENTH
CENTURY

54. *For the Chippendale-furnished Edenton Bedroom at the Museum of Early Southern Decorative Arts, Brunschwig & Fils has reproduced a mid-eighteenth century chinoiserie wallpaper. Such combinations of Chinese figures, birds, flowers, and delicate ribbons were very popular in France as well as in the American colonies. Airy, repeated patterns were less overpowering than Chinese scenic wallpapers, and more adaptable to occidental rooms. Edenton, one of North Carolina's few ports, was the colonial capital of the Province for a time, and remained the cultural and social center of its area. Here fifty-one ladies promised, at the famous Edenton Tea Party in 1774, to drink no more tea and to wear no British-made cloth.*

There was an obvious difference of texture and height between the painted background and the paper mounted on it, and the problem was to blend the two into a unified whole. This was done with layer after layer of clear lacquer, each coat allowed to dry for twenty-four hours and sanded before the next coat was applied. As many as fifty or sixty coats might be required to submerge a thick wallpaper motif completely beneath an absolutely smooth and even surface.

The French method was not new; it had first been used in Venice to ornament furniture. Lacquered Venetian furniture of the sixteenth and early seventeenth centuries, unmatched for delicate design, was decorated with hand painting by famous artists (and their apprentices) for the palazzi of the city's merchant princes. At this time, Venice led all Europe as a center of printing, and a new craft evolved—a cut-paper imitation of hand painting which was called *lacche del uomo povero*, or "poor man's lacquer." It consisted of hand-coloring a print, cutting out elements of the design, gluing them to a lacquered cabinet, commode, secretary, or chair, and covering the whole with many coats of clear lacquer to blend the paper decoration and the painted background beneath a perfectly smooth surface. Occasionally, such furniture was so beautifully executed that it could be passed off as hand-painted, and such pieces were sold as the work of artists rather than of artisans.

Découpure, the art of cutting and pasting paper, flourished in France during the eighteenth century. At the court of Louis XVI, noble ladies including Marie Antoinette enjoyed cutting delicate scenes and patterns from white paper and pasting them over pale blue silk; these were gallic counterparts of the English papyrotamia and paper lace. They also decorated trays, screens, boxes, window shades and fans with pastoral scenes and Chinese motifs cut from contemporary prints and textiles. Soon they were cutting away all background around and within the motifs, and combining portions of several prints into composite designs. So great was the demand for suitable pictures that enterprising printers began to reproduce especially for découpure the designs of Boucher, Redouté, Watteau, and Jean Pillement, a master of chinoiserie whose birds, flowers, arabesques and vignettes were especially favored by the cult of cut-and-paste. Only twenty-six coats of varnish were required for these thinner papers—an obvious advantage.

Découpure

In 1760, découpure was described in English by Robert Sayer in his *Ladies' Amusement, or the Whole Art of Japanning Made Easy*. The large book contained no less than fifteen hundred hand-colored motifs borrowed from the designs of famous British and French artists—enough to keep a lady amused with cutting and pasting for a lifetime. According to Sayer's directions, seven finishing coats of clear varnish were the minimum requirement, but twelve were recommended; a final polish could be achieved by rubbing the varnished surface with rottenstone.

NINETEENTH-
CENTURY
DECOUPAGE

For some inexplicable reason, découpure traveled to the British Isles and the American continent under the assumed name of *decoupage*. It was closer in appearance to its oriental model than painted japan-work, but its many required coatings and sandings did not appeal to busy American women of the post-Revolutionary period.

During the Victorian era, however, a modified form of decoupage gained wide acceptance in England and the United States. This involved pasting a square, round, or oblong picture on a wooden box-top, outlining it with gold braid, and giving wood, braid and picture six to ten coats of clear varnish. Since the braid covered the edge of the picture, the textural difference between wood and paper was not noticeable; the varnished braid took on the appearance of a gilded frame.

POTICHOMANIA

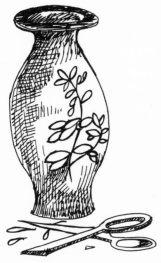

In the first half of the nineteenth century, the fad for still another sort of cut-paper craft work spread from France to England and the United States. *Potichomania* derived its name from the French *potiche*, meaning "an oriental vase," and *manie*, meaning "craze;" the craft consisted of pasting colored cut-motifs on the inside of clear glass vases and globes in imitation of Chinese or Sèvres porcelain. Any glass object with an opening large enough to admit the hand could be used. Motifs (especially butterflies, birds, and flowers) colored and cut from prints or engravings were attached to the inner surface with a very thin coating of mucilage. When the glue dried, the back of the paper cutout was sealed with shellac; over this and the entire inner surface, two or three coats of colorful paint were applied. Seen through the curved glass of the container, the paper ornamentation had a depth and a glow that were very desirable. Vases decorated in this way were filled with sand and used as mantel ornaments; globes were used over the clear glass chimneys of kerosene lamps.

A variation on this technique was the Dolly Varden jar. Tinted cutouts were pasted on the outside of a solid-color glass or china vase, and coated with clear varnish for protection; such a vase was used as a flower container.

CONTEMPORARY
DECOUPAGE

Small wooden boxes still are often decorated with a print or a pattern cut from wallpaper, and finished with a wooden frame. This can be a ready-made picture frame; it can also be made of narrow half-round molding, cut to size and mitred at the corners at the builder's supply company where it is purchased. As an alternative to the frame, the edge of the picture may be covered with cloth braid, which comes in many colors including gold and silver, from a cloth shop or the notions counter of a department store. Clear household cement is used to affix either the wood frame or the braid border.

Ornamenting boxes, screens, chests, table tops and trays with cutout and recombined paper motifs is an even more popular form of contemporary craft work. It is not necessary that all elements of a projected découpage design be taken from a single print, but all papers should be of similar thickness and texture. For instance, several documentary wallpaper samples might contribute birds, tree-limb sections, and foliage for an Audubon-type "print"; two or three old architectural engravings could be combined to form a street scene in grisaille; glossy surfaced seed-catalog illustrations might be incorporated into a graceful bouquet. The design

55. *Done by an expert, decoupage can be as intricate and beautiful as this detail from a wardrobe door decorated early in the twentieth century by Caroline King Duer. Hundreds of motifs, each cut separately and mounted individually on the wooden panel, are combined with great artistry in the hanging basket and its floral frame. Many layers of clear varnish meld the paper and its painted background beneath an absolutely smooth surface. This outstanding example of decoupage is from the collection of the Cooper-Hewitt Museum of Design, Smithsonian Institution, in New York City.*

should be planned with the shape and size of the surface to be decorated in mind, for scale is of the utmost importance. Very sharp scissors are essential. Several pairs, in different sizes, with straight or curved blades (manicure, embroidery, buttonhole) may be used to advantage, as well as library shears for cutting pictures apart before trimming begins.

Varnish, even the "colorless" variety, yellows slightly as it dries, and the many coats required for decoupage finish will change pure white to ivory and give blues a greenish cast. If true pastel shades are important, there are new plastic and fiberglass finishes especially made for use over paper, and they do remain clear. These products are available, with directions for their use, in large artist's supply shops.

Most practitioners of the art of decoupage remain wedded to the traditional varnish-and-sandpaper finish, which gives dimensional depth to a design rather than a glassy look. To minimize the jaundicing caused by varnish, they find black a safe background color, and often choose prints in reds, yellows, and greens.

MAKING A DECOUPAGE DESIGN

If the top of an oblong wooden cigarette box is to be decorated with decoupage, begin by giving the whole box three coats of flat enamel of the desired background color. A miniature floral arrangement, eighteenth century in feeling, in an urn container would be an attractive and challenging design; look·for the pictured container first, in magazine advertisements or illustrated catalogs. Once it has been chosen, select flowers to fill it; be sure the flowers are correct in scale for the size of the container, and that their paper background is similar to that of the vase. Nurserymen's catalogs and magazine illustrations provide a wide selection of flower forms.

Cut out the picture of the container roughly, with shears, and trim its edges very carefully with smaller scissors. Hold the paper horizontal, in the left hand, moving it slowly to feed its edge into the blades of the scissors; the right hand, holding the scissors, does not move, but the right thumb opens and closes the blades. Cut out and trim each flower, individually, by the same method. Often it is easier to cut stems and leaves separately and to reunite them with the flower during the pasting process.

Before beginning to paste, try out the arrangement on the box lid, working as though making an arrangement of live flowers. Locate the container first. Set background spike material in place; add heavier flowers for a center of interest, and finally fillers of small blossoms and foliage. When you are satisfied with the arrangement, mark the position of the container, in chalk, on the painted box. Number the important flowers (on the back) and mark their positions. Paste in the same order, beginning with the container. Remember that elements of the design must not overlap. If a flower is to extend down over the lip of the container, place it on the container, outline it, and cut out the outline. Then, in pasting, fit the flower into its prepared socket. Edges of flowers should be butted but not lapped; each lap is an extra layer of paper that will require several more coats of varnish to obliterate. Apply a thin layer of white glue to the back of the paper with a small artist's brush, being sure that the edges are well coated. Center the vase on its marks, and press it down—on a large piece, this could best be done with a paint roller, but on a small boxtop a toy rolling pin will work very well. Wipe away any glue that oozes from beneath the edges of the paper with a dampened sponge. If a wrinkle appears, and does not yield to the rolling pin, slit the raised paper with a razor blade, add a small amount of glue (with a flat toothpick) under each edge of the cut, and apply pressure with a damp sponge. Then glue and place the background material, foreground flowers, and fillers. Remove any remaining chalk marks with a damp sponge.

When the paste-up is complete and the glue is thoroughly dry, pour out a small pool of fast-drying clear varnish in the center of the box lid; immediately spread it out to the edges with rapid, even strokes of a soft brush. Cover the box with an inverted cardboard carton (to keep off dust) and allow the varnish to dry for twenty-four hours. Rub the entire surface lightly with fine sandpaper (400) wrapped around a small block of wood. Wipe away the dust with a damp sponge, and dry with a soft cloth. Repeat this process until painted background and pasted decoration are indistinguishably blended—from ten to twenty coats of varnish will be required, depending upon the thickness of the paper. Extend the three final coats to cover the sides of the box as well as the top, and finish the whole box with an application of white wax furniture polish, lightly buffed.

IX
CRAFTS
AND TOYS
FROM
PLANTS

"Corn" was, of course, the all-inclusive name for grain-bearing plants but Indian corn or maize, destined to become the mainstay of the settlers' diet, was unlike any grain that Europeans had even seen. From friendly Indians, the colonists obtained seed-corn, and learned to plant five kernels together in a small mound—"one for the cutworm, two for the crow, one to wither and one to grow"—and to bury a dead fish, for fertilizer, in each hill. They learned to roast ears of green corn in the husk by burying them in hot ashes. The mature kernels were parched and eaten with salt, ground into meal in a log mortar, or turned into hominy with lye obtained from wood ashes.

Indian women made bread of cornmeal mixed with bear-grease and baked it, in a thick cake, on a flat stone covered with an inverted clay bowl. Over the bowl, glowing coals were heaped, and the bread baked quickly in this primitive oven. Colonial women made this unleavened bread in a long-handled iron skillet with a domed cover; this "Dutch oven" was placed in the heart of the fire and covered with hot coals. For even quicker cooking, cornmeal mixed with grease and water was patted out into a thin cake on a moistened slab of wood. The breadboard was leaned against the inside wall of the fireplace, and the dough baked in the reflected heat of the flames. This bread was hard and crusty and kept well, so it often was prepared for travellers; for this reason it was called a *journey cake,* and the name was corrupted to "johnny cake."

Corn Ears of corn were handsome things—long and slender, pebbled with kernels that usually were yellow but were sometimes streaked or splotched with orange, black, or red. Multicolored ears, strung up beside the kitchen fireplace, were instant decorations and could, in an emergency, be ground into meal. Stubby ears of strawberry corn, each kernel a tiny shiny-red bead, were grown especially for ornamental use. These were hung in clusters on the wall, or heaped in a basket or a bowl, with graceful branching dried corn-tassels added for interest. Sometimes the pale yellow husks of strawberry corn, dampened with water to make them pliable, were curled like the petals of a flower around the base of the beaded ear.

Peppers When Columbus sailed westward to find a new route to India, he was seeking seasonings rather than gold. At that time, fresh meat kept well only in the coldest weather; during the rest of the year, it often was half-spoiled before it reached the kitchen. Spices could overcome the odor of

56. *Maize ears occasionally had black, orange or red kernels, like the one at upper left. At husking bees, any man who found such an ear was entitled to a kiss from the girl of his choice. Small ears of shiny strawberry corn were grown especially for decoration, and their husks were curled in a flower. In the left foreground is a shuck flower; the husks of the strawberry ear at top right are untreated. Popcorn kernels (in the foreground) are small, pointed ovals, quite unlike the flat, shield-shaped grains of field corn which have been shellacked and strung, Indian fashion, into this necklace, from the Arrowcraft Shop, Gatlinburg, Tennessee.*

decay, and black pepper could disguise the taste, but these cooking aids came to Europe only from the Orient. Although Columbus failed to find India or the Spice Islands, he did discover hot pod-peppers in the West Indies. When he returned to Spain in 1493, he took along samples of peppers and seeds, and their culture rapidly spread to other European countries.

Later explorers found the North American continent liberally supplied with pod-peppers that ranged in taste from fresh to fiery—red and green, of course, but also white, yellow, violet and brown. To sailors who had spent weeks at sea without fresh fruits or vegetables, sweet green peppers tasted like ambrosia. They, and the settlers who followed them, ate bell peppers raw, without salt, and relished them as much as apples.

The Indians used dried pepper pods, both sweet and hot, as seasonings for meat stews and the colonists did likewise. A string of red hot-peppers hung beside the fireplace in every seventeenth-century kitchen, to be used

57.   *On the chimney breast in the separate kitchen building at the Blount Mansion in Knoxville, herbs and red peppers hang within reach of the cook, but also serve to decorate the room. Tiny ears of strawberry corn are purely ornamental; slender yellow ears of popcorn wait to be shelled and popped.*

not only in soups and stews but also in cooking nourishing but rather tasteless squash. Peppers retained their glowing colors as they dried in the warm, dim kitchen, and the most universal of early wall decorations was the string of ornamental peppers of various hues.

Gourds   Gourds had been cultivated by the Indians long before the first Europeans arrived in North America. They grew in various sizes, shapes, and colors, and the settlers learned to use them in many different ways. First their shells had to be dried. This was done by piercing them at both ends with an awl, turning them once a day, and daily wiping accumulated moisture from their surfaces with a cloth. The drying period lasted from two to three weeks, depending upon the size of the gourds and the thickness of their shells.

The large round Pumpkin-gourd had its top cut off after drying, and its seeds removed; the resulting thin, tough curved shell made a splendid bowl. Long-handled Dipper-gourds were indispensible for scooping water out of a deep barrel, a shallow stream, or a small spring; they also were used as ladles and as measures. A round, short-handled gourd with a small hole cut near the top could be hung on the wall to store a single variety of precious seed from harvest to spring planting time; the row of Seed-gourds served a decorative purpose on the kitchen wall. The name "Bottle-gourd" conjures up a picture of this variety with its slender neck topping a large, flat-bottomed and bulbous hollow base. By cutting off the hollow neck two or three inches above the swelling, a fine flask was obtained, and a section of corncob was used as a stopper. From the tough, dried pith of the Dishrag-gourd, scouring pads were made. Little ovid Simling-gourds were exactly right in size and shape for nest-eggs and were handy, too, for darning stockings. As their shells dried, the seeds of gourds became loose and could be shaken free of the interior pith. Gourd rattles, with stick handles, were used by many Indian tribes in ceremonial dances, keeping time to the rhythm of the drums and punctuating the tuneless chants. A large Simling-gourd, mounted on a short wooden handle, was the early-American baby's rattle.

Small, bright-colored or warted gourds served then as now for decoration. Dried and polished with oil or beeswax, they were heaped in a basket or gathered into a string for hanging on the kitchen wall.

58. *Ingenious pioneers found many uses for the inedible gourds which grew in such variety of shapes and sizes. At upper left, a tiny bottle gourd becomes a posy holder. Beside the child's egg basket of willow splits is a simling-gourd, right in shape and size for a nest egg or a darning egg. The seeds of dried gourds loosened from the pith and struck against the thin shell with considerable clatter; in the center is a baby's rattle with a wooden handle, made from a large simling. A doll with a painted simling-gourd head and cotton hair leans against a century-old dipper-gourd—its handle is thirty-three inches long. These are arranged on an early nineteenth century hand-woven woolen coverlet. The doll is from the Craft Center, Gatlinburg, Tennessee.*

Pumpkin and Squash   Squash and pumpkins, to which the colonists also were introduced by the Indians, were edible cousins of the serviceable gourd, and they too had decorative uses. After the pulp of a large pumpkin had been scraped out for cooking, its shell could be sun-dried for a bowl; the thin tough shell darkened as its moisture evaporated to an orange-mottled brown. Squash of all kinds had interesting shapes; the Crook-neck, Patty-pan, and Acorn varieties were often arranged in a basket and served a turn as kitchen ornaments while waiting to be cooked.

BASKET WEAVING

The original basket makers were birds, and basket-weaving—one of the most ancient of all arts—has been the spontaneous invention of primitive peoples in all parts of the globe. European explorers found some American Indians living in houses made by weaving supple saplings in and out of rows of upright posts, and carrying heavy loads in burden baskets made of splinted wood. Smaller storage baskets were graceful in shape and often were woven in colorful patterns or decorated with shells, pebbles and feathers. The thing that most surprised the white men was that Indians could, and did, substitute baskets for so many articles that Europeans made of metal or of wood. Captain John Smith wrote in wonder that Indians in Virginia carried basket shields and wore basket armor so tightly woven that an arrow could not penetrate it. Indians carried water in baskets coated with tree-gum, and floated down rivers in basket boats caulked with pine pitch. They cooked in clay-lined baskets, filling them with water and dropping in hot stones to make the water seethe, and sifted cornmeal through basket sieves. They wove sturdy sandals, and basket hats for protection from sun and rain.

By trade or purchase, the colonists acquired baskets from the Indians, but they developed special shapes of their own for specific uses—for example, the egg-basket that was flat on one side. It could be hung on the wall until filled, and then was attached to a saddle for the trip to market, fitting safely against the shoulder of the horse. One pioneer "invention" was actually a rediscovery: the reed bread-raising basket, filled with dough and wrapped in a cloth, stood overnight on the warm hearth. In shape, construction, and material this was almost identical to baskets found in early Egyptian tombs.

Honeysuckle Baskets   Sedge, cornhusks, willow wands, cattail leaves, river cane, and honeysuckle vines all made good baskets. The long supple runners of honeysuckle were gathered when the sap was down, then wound into balls, dropped into hot water, and boiled for four hours; then the bark was peeled away and the withes were soaked in cold water overnight. The next morning, they were rinsed and hung to dry in the sun. After each small knot had been removed with a knife, the weaving could begin. An uneven number of spokes were tied together and separated into a flat circle. Beginning at the center, long canes were woven in and out of the spokes, and the work went fast. To shape the sides of the basket, the spokes were dipped in hot water and bent to the desired angle; the weaving continued until the basket attained the wanted depth. To finish the top, the ends of the spokes were wetted once again, and bent down; their tips were woven into the last row of cane, on the inside of the rim, and this created a flat scalloped edge. Handles were added by twisting several dampened vines

59. *The Qualla Indian Reservation in western North Carolina adjoins the Great Smoky Mountains National Park. Here Cherokee women make stunning baskets of stripped, split river cane; twenty canes the size of fishing poles are required for each one. Some of the weaving canes are dyed a rich black by boiling them for eight hours with freshly-dug walnut roots that have been pounded to powder with a sledge hammer.*

together, spreading the loose ends apart, and threading each tip downward through the woven side. Baskets made in this manner were used in colonial homes as containers for everything from kindling wood to flowers.

"Splits" of white oak, hickory, ash, or buckeye were sturdy basket ma- *Split Baskets* terials. The wood was cut when the sap was up; it was quartered, and split with the grain into thin strips which were soaked in water to make them pliable. Indian burden baskets of white oak splits were carried on the back, but the settlers made their market baskets with a single handle across the center, to be grasped in the palm or laid across the forearm. In standard sizes, split baskets became units of measurement that have persisted in the bushel and the half-bushel. There were unusual shapes for specified uses; for instance, the tall peach basket, much wider at the top than at the bottom, whose sides helped bear the weight of successive layers of fruit.

The fronds of the palmetto tree that grew so rapidly in South Carolina and Georgia were almost circular in shape, and had only to be trimmed to

60. *Walnut roots were also used by the Cherokee to color thin wood splits, from which sturdy burden baskets were made. When the sap rose, an oak, hickory, or buckeye sapling was selected, cut down, and quartered. Then the wood was split with the grain into long thin splints, which were soaked in water (to make them pliable) before being woven. These two modern carryalls, of white-oak splits, have been woven in typical Cherokee decorative patterns.*

61. *Basketry is a craft practiced by many members of the Southern Highland Handicraft Guild. Among these gifted basket makers are Cherokee Indians and descendants of the early settlers in this mountainous area; the ancient art has been handed down through many generations to present-day craftsmen. Basket dyes were made of various roots and barks, particularly of walnut, willow, oak, and sassafras. Tough, supple honeysuckle runners, of which these three colorful examples are woven, were gathered when the vines were dormant, coiled, and boiled four hours to soften the bark for removal; then they were soaked overnight in water and hung in the sun to dry. Knots were removed with a sharp knife.*

62. *In the collection of Fort Acres, at Boscawen, New Hampshire, are these two chairs with seats hand-woven of native plant materials. On the ladder-back chair, soaked rushes have been used to create an interesting pattern in which four triangles form the four side sections of a rectangle. The basket-woven seat of the low-back rocker is made of inner-bark hickory splints.*

a handy size to become palm-leaf fans. Each frond, moreover, was composed of narrow strips that could easily be split apart for plaiting into baskets, or wide-brimmed hats to protect against the hot summer sun.

Chair Seats The same materials used to make baskets could be woven into chair seats and footstool tops. By twisting rushes together into a slender rope, and winding this rope over and under the chair's wooden side supports, a warp was created. The weft was first tied around the back bar at one corner, then was woven in and out of the warp rushes, and was looped over the front support to begin the passage in the opposite direction. By this method, white oak or hickory splits could be woven into seats for the typically American kitchen chairs with short slat backs.

CORNSHUCK CRAFTS The colonists learned very early that cornshucks, dampened for pliability and twisted together for length and strength, could be woven or spiral-looped across a chair-seat frame. Shuck-bottomed chairs were as stout as the split-bottomed variety, and far more decorative. Split shucks were woven into baskets, or plaited into hats. Whole husks were braided into doormats and horse-collars. If feathers for bed-ticks were not available, corn shucks provided a rustling, lumpy mattress filling. Even the corncob was not exempt from the craftsman's busy fingers: reamed out and fitted with a hollow willow stem, the cob end became a tobacco pipe.

WHITTLING Making small useful articles of wood with no tool other than a whetstone-sharpened knife was "wet weather work" for the settlers, and whittling was an occupation they greatly enjoyed. A man took pride in making a neat long-handled cooking spoon, a well-fitted door latch, or a smooth shuttle of dogwood for the family loom. He might spend hours in carving an intricate pattern on a butter mold, and feel the time well spent whenever he saw the design imprinted on a pat of yellow butter at the table.

Colonial housewives envied the close-grained bowls that Indians made from maple burls, but obliging husbands found them hard to copy. Maple was a hard wood, difficult to whittle, and the grain of a burl ran in every direction. The settlers were forced to resort to the Indian trick of burning out the center of the bowl with hot coals, but days of whittling, burning, scraping and sanding still were required to complete the project. When the bowl's veined and mottled surface was oiled and polished, it was indeed a thing of beauty that seemed well worth the trouble.

HOMEMADE TOYS Sometimes a father whittled for pure pleasure, making a diminutive chest or a jointed wooden "puppet" for his little girl. The head, neck and trunk of a doll usually were carved from a single block of wood. Arms and legs, shaped from sticks, were attached with wooden dowel pins at shoulder and hip. Sometimes pegged elbow and knee joints were added, so that the doll could sit alone in a toy chair.

Imaginative children saw toys in all sorts of everyday objects. Most bedsteads were corded—that is, rope was laced across the frame in lieu of springs—and after a time the cords stretched. They then were tightened with a wooden wrench, shaped like a gigantic clothespin with a straight bar inserted crosswise near the knobbed top for a turning handle. These bed-wrenches did look like crude human figures, and the "heads" were sometimes given carved or painted features. They were a household necessity but were not needed daily; between times, they made fine boy

63. *Members of the Southern Highland Handicraft Guild produce many useful and ornamental things from cornhusks—chair seats, door mats, baskets, belts, sun hats, and shopping bags—but nothing more charming than character dolls. This hunter, his gun, and his hound-dog are all made of shucks; some are in natural yellow-tan, while others have been dyed for attractive color contrast.*

64. *In Salem, Massachusetts, the Essex Institute's collection of historical photographs includes a number of early day playthings. This group of dolls shows: (1) a cornhusk woman dressed for church in a bonnet trimmed with tiny cornhusk flowers; (2) a jointed wooden doll with a composition head, dressed in high-waisted Empire style; (3) an undressed doll whose carved wooden head, arms, and legs are attached to a stuffed kid-skin body; (4) a pocket-size carved wooden doll, with painted face and hair.*

dolls. Whittled clothes-pegs that held heavy laundry on the clothesline were kept in a basket when not in use, and many a one disappeared to become an armless doll. Later, smaller wooden clothespins were commercially produced. Dolls made from these were very appealing and just pocket size; they were given matchstick arms and painted faces.

The pesky cockleburrs that clung to clothing would also stick to each other. Children built tiny beds and chairs of these for clothes-peg dolls, and tables to be set with acorn cups.

The miraculous maize plant produced toys for colonial children as well as food, and useful articles for their elders. The settlers' sons duelled with cornstalk swords, jousted with pointed cornstalk spears, and fought sham battles with cornstalk guns. Slices of corncob served as wheels for their toy wagons, and as counters for their games.

SHUCK DOLLS   The colonists' daughters began to make corn "puppets" for themselves. Sometimes they gave a corncob body a hickory nut head, legs and arms of sticks, and cornshuck clothes. More often, they discarded the cob entirely; by tying husks with narrow strips of shuck, they could create a legless doll with wide skirts. Several shucks were dampened and folded together at

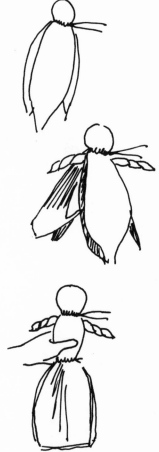

the middle; a strip of shuck was wound around the whole bundle near the top, and tied to form a neck. A slim roll of husk, inserted between the halves of the folded bundle beneath the neck, formed the doll's arms; below this, a second winding and tying with a shuck strip made an indentation for the waist, and the loosely flaring layered shuck ends were evenly trimmed into skirt and petticoats. Cornsilk hair, glued on with the natural adhesive provided by the gum-tree, finished the head, and features were drawn on the face with a charred stick.

As time passed, other more sophisticated dolls were made or bought for little girls, but none supplanted the shuck doll which a child could make herself. Fashions changed, and the dolls changed with them. Bonnets, kerchiefs, and aprons were easily cut from husks and glued or tied in place. Fewer shucks in the bundle and a higher waistline gave a doll the Empire look; feathers or shuck flowers atop her cornsilk hair provided a period headdress. Even leg o' mutton sleeves, parasols, and picture hats, in their turn, were reproduced in cornhusks. Although the heads and bodies of shuck dolls were most often left in their natural pale straw color, shucks were dyed for clothing and for hats.

65. *In colonial times, dolls often were given heads of hickory nuts; the pointed nut tips made natural noses, and wrinkles and pits on the shells could be painted to resemble features. In the extensive collection of the Essex Institute in Salem, Massachusetts, is this group of rag dolls with hickory-nut heads busily at work around a quilting frame. Their ladder-back chairs of whittled sticks are put together with wooden pegs.*

66. *As styles of dress changed, corn-husk dolls' clothes followed the fashion. This buxom turn-of-the-twentieth-century lass wears old leg o'mutton sleeves and carries a long-handled parasol. A tiny hat, with a cornshuck bird of paradise, is perched on her flowing cornsilk hair, and her short cape is tied beneath her chin in a large bow. This fascinating period piece is from the doll collection of the Denver Art Museum.*

From time immemorial, soft rag dolls have been loved by little girls. At **RAG DOLLS** first, the small daughters of the colonists made dolls of deerskin, since cloth was too valuable to be spared for "play-pretties," and stuffed them with dried sweet grass or aromatic balsam needles. The cloth dolls that very soon replaced these "Indian babies" were stuffed with milkweed down. Small egg-shaped simling gourds were pale beige in color, and made fine heads for dolls. Features were drawn or painted on, and strands of corn-silk or tufts of wool were glued on for hair. The stem of the gourd (or a sharp stick punched through the end of the shell) served as the doll's neck, and the cloth body was gathered and tied around it. When cotton became plentiful, dolls made of unbleached domestic were stuffed with cotton bat-ting and dressed in printed calico; they had yarn hair, and shiny shoe-button eyes. Often the doll was child-size, and wore the cast-off garments of her owner.

Sometimes small rag dolls were given apple heads. A peeled Russet **APPLE DOLLS** apple was placed in the sun to dry. As its moisture evaporated, the sur-face began to shrivel. By judicious pinching with the fingers, a nose and chin could be formed; eye sockets were made more pronounced by press-ing them in with the thumb. Daily the features were pinched and pressed, until the flesh of the apple was completely dry and no longer malleable. Then the apple head was impaled on a pointed stick which was inserted into the stuffed cloth body of the doll; the neck opening was gathered around the stick and tightly tied in place. As time passed, the dried apple head became hard and leathery to the touch; it also darkened to a leather brown.

In recent years, apple heads have been given only to character dolls; the wrinkled texture and dark color seem just right for the weather-beaten face of a sea-captain or of an ancient crone. Doll makers find it better to carve the features while the apple still is firm, and a wire armature usually replaces the stick neck and cloth body that were formerly preferred. Small armatures (intended as the basis for modelling statuettes) may be bought in some hobby shops and in large artist's supply houses; they can be made at home by bending two lengths of coathanger wire, one long and one short, together at the middle; wrapping the bundle for one inch with plastic tape creates a neck. The two short wire ends become arms. The two long ends are wrapped together for the length of the body, and then are separated into legs. The finished armature has the look of a stick-figure without a head.

Golden Delicious apples have been found especially suited to doll making, for the firm flesh wrinkles little as it dries, and retains its light beige color well. A medium-sized apple is first pared with a thin sharp knife, so care-fully that no ridges remain. Eyes, nose and mouth are then carved with the tip of the knife—as the apple shrinks in drying, the features will be altered and exaggerated, so that the finished face becomes a caricature of the sculptured original. The carved apple will dry naturally, in a warm room, in about three weeks. It is possible, however, to hasten the drying process and to obtain permanent light color at the same time. The carved apple should be dipped in fresh lemon juice (or in a solution of one table-spoonful of powdered citric acid dissolved in one cup of water) and placed

67.   *This wizened apple doll, made by Eunice Ellis for Dorothy Stykes of Akron, Ohio, is dressed in black bombazine with white net kerchief and cap. As apple heads de- hydrate, the carved features are altered; here the cheeks are puffed and wrinkled, while the mouth has shrunk to give the face a toothless look. The blue bead eyes were poked in gradually, a bit each day, until they were firmly set; the ridges which developed in the process have created the impression of eyelids.*

at once in the oven at a temperature of 150°. It should be kept at this low steady temperature for twenty-four hours, and is then ready for mounting.

If a wire armature is used, a hole must be bored in the blossom end of the apple before drying; the neck of the armature, dipped in white glue, is fitted into the hole when the dehydrating process is complete. Meanwhile, the arms, legs, and body of the armature have been wrapped very tightly with narrow strips of cloth secured with plastic tape, until the desired shape and proportion have been obtained. Although some doll makers like to paint the apple faces and to glue bead eyes in the sockets, the untouched heads are very lifelike. Hair, made of cotton batting or raw wool, is glued on and topped with a bonnet, a lace cap, or a hat. When the doll is appropriately dressed, it becomes not a toy but a conversation piece.

Fresh apples have for centuries been used as decorations. Polished and arranged in a bowl, they delight the eye with color while their delicate scent perfumes a room. The pleasant fragrance of apples was especially appreciated in colonial times, when the smoke and smell of cooking permeated the entire house.

POMANDERS

To counteract noxious odors, in city streets as well as indoors, pomanders had been winter replacements for the nosegay of flowers that Elizabethan ladies carried with them everywhere. As the name implies, pomanders were made of apples, selected for their natural perfume and their keeping qualities. The unpeeled fruit was pierced all over with a small sharp-pointed twig, and the stem of a whole clove was inserted in each hole; enough cloves were used to cover the apple completely. As it dried, and for many months thereafter, the pomander gave off a spicy, cidery scent. Dehydrating pomanders were arranged in a row on a shelf or a sunny window sill, and served as decorations while freshening the air. When completely dry, they were heaped in a basket on a table in the keeping room, to be convenient for individual use. A pomander, warmed in the hands, was held beneath the nose and sniffed as necessary.

When the atmosphere of houses and streets grew pleasanter, pomanders did not entirely disappear; they merely moved to the linen shelf or the clothes closet. In the nineteenth century, it became customary to roll the pierced apple in powdered orris root before inserting the cloves, and the tines of a fork replaced the sharpened stick for piercing the skin. Experimentation proved that other fruits could be used. In the South, where citrus fruits were available before they could be transported to other parts of the country, oranges and lemons were rolled in powdered cinnamon or allspice before being studded with cloves. Sweetest of all pomanders were the miniatures made of the tiny inedible fruit of the mock-orange.

Children have always enjoyed making pomanders, and do so today in clubs and scout troops. Adults who make them by the dozen, for gifts or for bazaars, find it helpful to use a thimble in pushing the cloves into the fruit. A loop of narrow ribbon, attached with a wire hairpin, makes a convenient hanger, and the fruit is unlikely to spoil if the pomander is conditioned as soon as it is made, by hanging it for two weeks in a cool, dry closet.

X
CANDLE CRAFTS

When we say that our ancestors worked from sunup to sundown, we are speaking the literal truth. After dark, with doors bolted and windows securely shuttered, colonial families gathered around the huge fireplace that was an invariable feature of the principal room. Flickering flames often provided the room's only light, and this did not penetrate to the shadowy corners.

With various crude devices, the early settlers sought to obtain more illumination. Some used the rushlight in which the pith of dried marsh grass was soaked in grease and placed in an iron "pincher" that served as a holder. The greasy rushes burned rapidly and gave off a great deal of smoke but very little light. Betty lamps, which had been used in ancient Greece and Rome, still were shaped like Aladdin's lamp in colonial times. The name derived from an old English word, *bettyngs,* meaning fat or oil, and the lamp was no more than a shallow metal dish filled with any available fats or meat drippings. Its oval shape was elongated to a lip at one end; a linen rag wick was immersed in the oil and laid along the lip, and the flame burned at its tip. Like rushlights, betty lamps were smoky, smelly, and inefficient.

The settlers discovered a simpler but pleasanter and brighter source of light in long thin strips of fat pine wood. Pitch pine, from which these slender torches were obtained, grew throughout the colonies; it was called "candle wood" in New England, and "lightwood" in the South. The pine slivers gave off a pleasant odor as they burned, but they also oozed sticky resin; for this reason, they were not placed about the room but were kept near the fireplace. A single stick of pine could be wedged upright between two hearthstones. Several slivers, burning at both ends in a wrought-iron basket, gave short-lived but very good illumination.

CANDLE MAKING IN THE SEVENTEENTH CENTURY

Preparing Tallow

During the seventeenth and eighteenth centuries, candles were the best means of illumination in the Old World and the New. They were of two kinds, wax and tallow, but burning expensive wax tapers was the prerogative of royalty, nobility, and the Church.

In England, candle tallow was made from the fat of sheep. In the colonies, where sheep were few, any sort of suet or animal grease—beef, pork, goose, deer, opossum, or bear, to name but a few—was used in candlemaking. Fats were carefully hoarded all year round, in a barrel. In the autumn, great masses of the rancid mixture were added to huge kettles of hot water, and were boiled and skimmed over and over until a clear tallow resulted. This unpleasant process took several days.

At first, candles were made entirely by the dipping method. In prepara- *Dipping Candles*
tion, two long parallel poles were set up in a cool place well away from the
fire—often in a lean-to shed. Across these poles the candle rods (slender
sticks about eighteen inches long) would rest. Each rod was hung with
six or eight wicks, depending upon the size of the tallow kettle; the middle
of a cord was folded over the rod, and the two ends were twisted together.

When the tallow had been melted in a large kettle, the housewife dipped
the wicks, a rodful at a time, into the pot. After dipping, the rod was
returned to the rack until the tallow had cooled and hardened. When the
last set of wicks had been dipped, it was time to begin again with the first
rod; the candles grew fatter as they were repeatedly dipped and cooled. It
was no easy matter to keep the contents of the kettle at the correct even
temperature, but it the tallow was too cool, the candle emerged from it
lumpy, and if it was too hot, it would melt off the layers that had already
been deposited on the wick. Once the candles were completely hardened,
the wicks were slipped off the rod, leaving a characteristic loop at the base of
each candle. In spite of the tedious clarification process, tallow candles
smoked and gave off the unpleasant smell of burning grease.

An expert candlemaker could produce only about two hundred "tallow-
dips" in a day of gruelling labor. The dips were carefully stored away in
a wooden chest where they were safe from mice. They were used sparingly,
for they would have to last until a new supply of tallow accumulated.

68. *This typical early eighteenth-century New England interior, displayed at the
Smithsonian Institution in Washington, D.C., shows simple handcrafted furniture
against a background of unpainted pine paneling. At that time, the shelves of a corner
cupboard held the family's most treasured pieces of china and pottery. In most homes,
an hourglass was the only timepiece. The double candleholder was a great convenience;
the bar was adjustable, and could be raised or lowered to a convenient height. The
characteristically small window has "bull's-eye" panes; all window glass made in the
colonies had similar glaring imperfections. This was not an imperfection as such but
an unavoidable result of the making of glass in sand molds.*

Candleholders were rare. The average household might boast one or two of carved wood or cast iron, but usually the candle was affixed in a wooden saucer (or to a shelf or table) by settling its base in a splotch of its own dripped tallow.

Lanterns

Lanterns were not new when Diogenes used one in his search for an honest man. In the colonial period, candle-lanterns lighted the belated traveller on his way, the watchman on his rounds, the farmer to the barn. The iron bull's-eye lantern was square, and had only one glazed side; this glass, like the windowpanes of the time, was green in color and showed a characteristic round and watery imperfection responsible for the lantern's name. Tin lanterns were round, with a hinged bottom centered by a candle-cup and a peaked top ending in a ring that could be slipped over the finger for carrying or used to hang the lantern inside the house. Like those still made in Mexico, they emitted light through holes punched in the thin metal with the point of a nail; the holes might be scattered or in vertical rows, but were more often arranged in a decorative pattern such as a sunburst.

Bayberry Candles

All along the eastern seacoast wild bayberry bushes grew in great profusion. It was a lucky day when some unknown New Englander first conceived the idea of gathering the waxy berries and boiling them down into clear greenish tallow. Bayberry candles had many advantages. First of all, the raw material was in abundant supply and free for the taking, and the berries could be gathered by children. The sage-green candles hardened beautifully and kept straight even in hot summer weather; they burned slowly, with a clear and steady flame. Last but certainly not least, they gave off a spicy fragrance!

It became the custom, when company was expected, to light a bayberry candle and then snuff it out; the drifting smoke perfumed an entire room. Travellers took back to England the news of the green candles that burned so bright and smelled so good, and before long the colonists were exporting as many bayberry candles as they could make.

CANDLES IN THE EIGHTEENTH-CENTURY

Metal candle molds were an early American labor-saving device. They were made of sheet iron, tin, or (occasionally) of pewter, in connected groups of slender, tapered tubes. Melted wax was poured into each tube, encasing a wick of twisted thread, and the mold was then set aside in a cool place. When the candles had hardened completely, the mold was dipped into hot water to release them; they were then lifted out of the tubes and polished with a soft cloth. Although tallow still had to be collected and clarified, molding candles seemed almost indecently easy to housewives accustomed to the laborious dipping process.

69. *Fort Acres, the oldest house in Boscawen, New Hampshire, was built about 1760 by the Reverend Roby Morrill; some of its beams probably came from a fort constructed in 1733 to protect the early settlers from hostile Indians. Among the many interesting articles grouped around its brick-oven fireplace are four types of colonial candleholders: a lantern with its original bottle-green bull's eye glass, a tall wrought-iron candlestand, a wrought-iron wall sconce, and an adjustable wooden light stand that held two candles. Such a stand was placed beside a chair for reading; its small table top held book and spectacles.*

70. *In 1926, John D. Rockefeller, Jr. undertook the preservation and restoration of an entire town, Colonial Williamsburg. This had been the capital of Virginia from 1699 to 1780, and a brilliant social life centered around the magnificent Governor's Palace from its completion in 1720 to its destruction by fire in 1781. By 1934, the Palace stood again on its original foundations; researchers were aided in its reconstruction by a floor plan drawn by Thomas Jefferson in 1779. In the Palace scullery, a candle is removed from a pewter mold by immersing the mold in hot water and gently pulling on the exposed wick at its base. Then the excess wick will be trimmed off, and the candle will be polished with a soft cloth.*

71. *In most colonial homes, small table-top candle molds were used. These three, of varied sizes, are from the extensive collection of the Bedford Historical Society in Bedford, New York. The candle wicks were tied to a rod laid across the top of the mold; one rests across the six-candle mold in the center.*

Women were much more liberal in the use of these new molded candles. Brass candlesticks (each with a short pointed spike on which the candle was impaled) and candleholders (ending in cups into which the base of a taper fitted) were placed on tables and tall candle-stands; in the homes of the wealthy, silver candelabra began to grace dining room tables and sideboards. Sconces were fixed to walls, and branched lighting fixtures were suspended from ceilings—for the finest houses, chandeliers of Waterford crystal, silver, or brass were imported, while in less elaborate settings sconces and chandeliers were carved or of turned wood. Wall and ceiling fixtures of wrought iron were popular for kitchens that doubled as dining rooms. Even in primitive, rustic homes there were hanging candleholders: crossed wooden boards with candle-cups carved out along their length; wooden wheels, hung horizontally, with candleholders around their rims; wrought iron candle-cups with long handles ending in hooks that could be slipped over a nail on the wall.

To welcome a royal governor, or to celebrate the king's birthday, town fathers often ordered an *illumination*. Every householder was expected to place a lighted candle in each window that faced the street, and any homeowner who did not comply was fined. Along the dark streets, rows of lighted houses made an impressive and festive sight, but housewives resented the custom for its wasteful use of their cherished candles. During the Revolutionary War, however, spontaneous illuminations heralded the news of each victory of the Continental Army.

During the Regency Period, the Prince of Wales (who would later become King George IV) had such a particular fondness for cut-crystal "drops" that a craze developed in England for huge prism chandeliers and large lusters. Americans, too, liked the look of crystal sparkling in candlelight, but they preferred to import (and to copy) lighter and more graceful chandeliers and girandoles from France.

The one great disadvantage of any candle was that the slightest puff of wind would blow it out; therefore the hurricane shade was hailed as a marvelous invention in the eighteenth century. This tall, bowed cylinder of clear glass fitted over the candle *and* its holder, and rested on the table-top; it was a thing of beauty as well as a convenience.

THE NINETEENTH CENTURY: CANDLES REPLACED BY ARTIFICIAL LIGHT

About 1800, a real improvement in lighting came with the invention, by Aime Argond, of a new kind of lamp. Air circulating inside its hollow wick caused whale oil to burn with a whiter, brighter flame. The Argond lamp was a far cry from the smoky betty lamp, and gave out as much light as several candles; it first became popular in France during the Empire Period, and its hollow base was classic in shape and made of bronze or tole.

Modification and improvement of the hollow-wick principle produced the Astral lamp, which was so constructed that no shadow was cast by the flattened, ring-shaped reservoir that contained the oil. Here at last, was a good, strong light for reading or for the fine embroidery that Victorian ladies did so well. Adults began to linger around the parlor table long after the children had been sent to bed, able for the first time in history to work comfortably by artificial light.

From the Pennsylvania coal fields came a plentiful new fuel, kerosene, that was commonly called "coal-oil," and both names were applied to the type of lamp in which it was burned. A wide woven wick, immersed in the oil that filled the hollow pressed-glass base, emerged through a slit in a metal mantle and the flame burned across its upper edge. By adjusting the height of the wick (with a screw on the outside of the mantle) the light could be dimmed or brightened. To protect the flame from wind, the lamp was topped with a clear glass chimney that borrowed the shape of the hurricane shade but was much smaller. In the gaslight era that spanned the second half of the nineteenth century, gas fixtures could be attached only to walls or to ceilings. People were used to portable light, so the kerosene reading lamp lingered on the parlor table while branching gas chandeliers and wall sconces were installed over and around it.

In spite of the fact that cleaning smoky lamp chimneys was an extra (and distasteful) chore, nineteenth-century housewives had welcomed the kerosene lamp as a tremendous advance in lighting and had accorded it a

72. *The clear glass hurricane shade that covered a candle and its holder was beautiful in its simplicity of form. However, it was not only decorative but also practical, for it protected the candle flame from drafts. At the Adam Thoroughgood House, near Norfolk, Virginia, a hurricane shade surrounds a candle in a tall silver candlestick. Through the glass, the edge of the winter bouquet of strawflowers, dried goldenrod and dock is plainly seen.*

place of honor on the parlor table. Once its novelty wore off, they looked at it critically. Practical it certainly was, but it *looked* utilitarian. Gradually, the table lamp became a decorative and a much decorated object. Manufacturers began to make bulbous china lamp-bases, and globe-shaped china shades that fitted over clear glass chimneys—this was the type of lamp called "Gone With the Wind" today. Ladies took one look at those smooth china surfaces and reached for a paintbrush; here was a perfect spot for hand painted roses, forget-me-nots, and still more roses!

Throughout the nineteenth century, in pioneer settlements and isolated areas not served by railroads, candles were used where kerosene was unavailable. The tin candle-mold was a household necessity in many a frontier home; in others, tallow dips were still made by seventeenth-century methods.

In 1901, the grounds and buildings of the Buffalo Exposition were illuminated with electricity, and people came from all over the world to marvel at the wonders of this first "flameless light." No matter how they were shaded, the first light bulbs gave off a garish and glaring light. The soft radiance of candle flames was especially flattering by comparison, and dining by candlelight (which had never really gone out of style) seemed romantic once it could be done by choice rather than of necessity. Colored candles appeared—pink ones to match a centerpiece of roses, or forget-me-not blue to emphasize patterned Haviland plates. Manufacturers, recognizing a trend, brought out red and green candles for the Christmas season. Candlesticks returned to mantels; candles in all sizes, shapes and colors were popular holiday decorations. Almost before women realized it, they were making candles again!

DECORATING WITH CANDLES IN THE TWENTIETH CENTURY

For the edification of a generation accustomed to and dependent upon electric light, candle-dipping is demonstrated in such large restorations as Old Sturbridge Village and Colonial Williamsburg, and at historic houses such as the Harlow Old Fort House in Plymouth, Massachusetts; hand-dipped candles are sold in restoration shops and at many house museums. Bayberry candles, like bayberry bushes, have become a rarity; they are sold as curiosities at specialty and museum shops.

MAKING CANDLES TODAY

For those who own, or have access to, colonial metal molds in good condition, molding candles in the eighteenth-century manner can be a fascinating form of craft work. The inner surface of each tube should be cleaned of all rust with a wire brush or a ball of steel wool wired to a slender stick.

Making Candles in Antique Metal Molds

73. *Fountain Elms, a Victorian mansion in the style of a Tuscan villa, was built in Utica, New York, in 1850 by James Watson Williams. In was restored in 1960, and is maintained by the Munson-Williams-Proctor Institute. On the Empire center table in the library, an elegant Astral reading lamp, with crystal prisms and frosted glass shade, sheds its shadowless light upon a brown wool table cover with applied yarn flowers. Beside the lamp is a rosewood reading stand, with a large round magnifying glass; a book was propped against the fretted back of the stand, and its print was magnified many times for the benefit of the myopic reader who sat before it.*

Thick 24-ply braided wicking can be bought at some hobby shops, but any heavy white cotton cord will serve the purpose. Any wax except pure beeswax may be used to fill the molds—at the Stephen Fitch House in Old Sturbridge Village, simulated tallow is made by combining five and a half pounds of paraffin with three pounds of Stearic acid and one pound of yellow beeswax.

Cut a wick for each tube of the mold, making it six inches longer than the tube itself. Tie a large knot at one end. Thread the untied end through the small hole in the base of the tube and bring it out at the top of the cavity. Tie the end of the wick around a pencil (or a skewer); rest the pencil across the top of the mold and twist it to wind the wick taut.

When all the tubes have been threaded with wicks, heat the wax slowly until just melted. Pour a tablespoonful of wax into each tube, to seal the knot of the wick; allow this to stand for a minute or two, and check the bottom of the mold for leaks. (If a tube is leaking, the wick must be removed and retied with a larger, tighter knot.) Place a small funnel in the top of a tube, and slowly pour melted wax through it until the cavity is filled. Recenter the wick. As the wax cools, probe each tube with a thin wire to free any trapped air bubbles. As the wax shrinks away from the sides of the tubes, pour in more melted wax; continue to add wax until there is no further shrinkage. Then allow the mold to stand in a cool place for at least three hours.

As the first step in unmolding, cut off the large knot at the base of each tube; the wax-covered cord will not yield to ordinary scissors, so it will be necessary to use tinsnips or a sharp knife. Immerse the whole mold in very hot water for about ten seconds. Lift a wick-wrapped pencil with a gentle, steady pull; the candle should slide slowly out. If it does not, re-dip the mold in hot water and try again. Trim off the long end of the wick, and polish the candle with a soft cloth.

MOLDING CANDLES
BY MODERN METHODS
Although candles are now sold in a great variety of sizes and in a veritable rainbow of colors, the craft of candle molding grows more popular with every passing year. Because wax shrinks as it hardens, almost any cylindrical or square hollow container may double as a mold, and any kind of wax except plain beeswax may substitute for simulated tallow. As anyone who has helped prepare for a charity bazaar can testify, candle-ends can be melted and remolded. Candles may also be made of pure paraffin, or of paraffin melted with candle-stubs.

Wax leaves a residue on the melting pot that is difficult to remove, so it is wise to use an old saucepan or, better yet, an old teakettle with a pouring spout. A small funnel helps to prevent spills while the mold is being filled. The wax should be heated very slowly, just until it becomes fluid; at this point, if candle-ends are being used, the wicks of the stubs will float to the surface and can be fished out with kitchen tongs.

An easy way to color candles is by melting wax crayons along with the paraffin or stubs; the wax should be stirred as it begins to melt, to distribute the color evenly. Wax also can be colored, after it is melted and removed from the heat, by stirring in lipstick or a few drops of artist's oil paint.

Scented candles are a delightful innovation reminiscent of the days of bayberry dips; as the candle burns, it perfumes an entire room. A few drops of oil of bayberry, oil of pine, or floral essence (all obtainable through a druggist) or a small amount of a favorite perfume may be used; solid cologne and scented bath oil also work exceedingly well. Melted wax should be removed from the heat and allowed to cool slightly before scent is added—in very hot wax, the perfume evaporates at once.

Using a Tin Can Mold

Round tin cans of all sizes, from two-ounce mushroom to thirty-two-ounce fruit juice, make fine molds; the candle can be made as tall as the can, or as short as you like. The tall square can that holds a pound of saltine crackers is another excellent possibility, and a short square candle often is an effective coffee-table decoration.

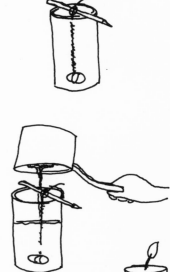

Wash the inside of the can with soap and warm water, rinse, and dry well. Rub the inner sides and bottom of the can lightly with mineral oil. Measure a wick of heavy white cotton cord, allowing an extra six inches; tie a curtain weight, a lead fishing sinker, or a small nail to one end of the wick. Drop the weighted end of the wick into the center of the can. Tie the loose end to a pencil laid across the can top, and wind the wick taut by turning the pencil.

Melt paraffin or candle-stubs slowly, removing the pan from the heat as soon as the wax is fluid. Add color with wax crayon, lipstick, or artist's oil paint. Cool slightly, and add perfume if desired. Using a funnel to prevent splashes and spills, pour the wax into the can. If you want a candle of a particular height, measure the inside of the can in advance, and mark the proper level with a scratch on the tin.

Place the can-mold in the refrigerator for several hours—the length of time required for complete hardening of the wax varies with the size of the candle. The wax will pull away from the sides of the can as it shrinks in hardening, and the candle is easily removed by turning the can upside down. If it does not slide out immediately, dip the can in hot water for a few seconds, turn it over, and tap the bottom with a hammer.

Trim the excess wick from the top of the candle, and polish the sides with a soft cloth. The large and handsome candle is then complete.

Molding a Candle in Glass

Hollow glass containers with straight sides, glass bowls, and glass vases wider at the top than at the base can also serve as molds; a glass mold must be rinsed in very hot water (to prevent cracking when the melted wax is poured in), dried, and lightly coated with mineral oil. Inserting the wick, preparing the wax, and filling the mold are done in the same way as for tin can molds, but the glass container should be allowed to cool for half an hour at room temperature before being placed in the refrigerator. The candle is removed by dipping the mold in hot water and pulling on the wick while the container is held upside down.

Any expendable glass bottle or jar (even one that is narrower at the top than at the bottom) can serve to mold one candle of unusual shape: those that came filled with wine, olives, vinegar, salad oil, or syrup are good possibilities. Wash the bottle very thoroughly, using a bottle brush and hot soapy water, drain, and allow it to dry completely. Lower a weighted wick into the center of the container; wind the excess wick on a pencil balanced across the mouth of the jar. Use a funnel to fill the container slowly with melted wax, colored and perfumed as you wish. Allow the bottle to stand at room temperature for half an hour, and then place it in the refrigerator until the candle is completely hardened. Then, with a glass-cutter, score the surface of the bottle four times, vertically, once on each side. Slip one large paper bag inside another, and place the scored bottle inside the double bag. Close and tie the end of the bag, lay it flat on a counter or table, and tap it sharply with a hammer. The glass will split along the cuts. Open the bag and carefully pull the sections of glass away from the candle; polish the candle with a soft dry cloth, and remove slight nicks by rubbing with a finger. For added interest, a raised pattern on such a candle may be highlighted with glue and a sprinkling of gold- or diamond-dust glitter.

Making a Lacy Candle　　The lacy candles sold in specialty shops may be produced at home by the following method: cut off the peaked top of a quart-size cardboard milk carton, and stand a ten-inch white candle upright in its center. Pack crushed ice between the candle and the sides of the carton, using enough ice to hold the taper straight and steady. Pour melted wax, colored with crayon, lipstick or oil-paint, over the ice to fill the container and cover all but the wick of the central candle. As the paraffin hardens, the ice melts and leaves its outline in empty spaces. When the wax has shrunk away from the cardboard, the candle has set; turn the container upside down and pour out the water. The candle should slide out with the water; if it does not, the cardboard can be peeled away, but this must be done gently lest the lacy edges break. When the wick is lighted, the center candle burns down inside the lacy lantern of its shell.

CONDITIONING MOLDED CANDLES

Whether they were shaped in colonial metal molds, tin cans, glass jars, or cardboard cartons, all handmade candles should be conditioned in a cool place for at least a week before being lighted. They can be stored in an unheated closet or in the hydrator drawer of a refrigerator, but should not be subjected to freezing temperatures. If they have not been conditioned, slender tapers tend to bend when placed in holders, and candles of all sizes burn too rapidly and give off more smoke.

DECORATING WITH MOLDED CANDLES

Attaching a Candle to a Base　　Many of the candles molded in cans or jars are too large to fit into conventional holders, and must be given bases of some other kind—a metal tray, a wooden plaque, or a china plate. To hold a tall candle steady, a heavy needlepoint flower holder is secured to the base with sticky floral tape, which is procurable from a florist. The end of the candle is softened slightly by moving it several times across a candleflame, turning it all the while, and is pressed down firmly on the points of the holder.

A seventeenth-century expedient works well for short, fat candles. Drip wax from a lighted candle on the base, and center the new candle on this wax while it still is warm.

Decorating the Base　　Handsome though a colorful and shapely candle is, it will look unfinished on a plain flat base. Live greenery, in the form of a wreath or a tapering spray, may be added and kept fresh for several days by inserting the stem ends in water-filled glass corsage tubes or in small blocks of soaked Oasis; both corsage tubes and Oasis may be obtained from a florist.

A more permanent, and very appropriate, trimming for the base would be a circlet or a spray of waxed live flowers and leaves. A wreath of short-stemmed fresh flowers is easily achieved by surrounding the candle on its tray or plaque with a glass ivy-ring filled with water.

Decorating with candles is a Christmas tradition that dates back to the *Decorating Large* Middle Ages. In the twentieth century, a flat wreath of laurel or holly, laid *Candles for Christmas* in place on a tray or plaque centered with a huge red candle, makes a striking centerpiece or coffee-table ornament. A single large bow of wide red velvet ribbon may be wired to a holly twig; several small bows of narrow red ribbon may be attached to laurel stems with "invisible" wire hairpins.

Even more effective as a surround for a fat red or green candle is the Della Robbia wreath, which begins with greenery laid flat on a plaque or tray. Small fresh or artificial fruits are placed upon the foliage and grouped by color; nuts, cones, seedpods, and bright berries may be added as accents.

More troublesome to make is a wreath of seed pods, nuts and cones, but it has the advantage of being a permanent decoration that can be used year after year. On a flat wreath form of white styrofoam plastic, the woody materials are mounded into a circlet of considerable width and depth. Clear household cement is used to bond a first layer of large nuts and flat cones to the plastic base. After this cement has dried, layer after layer of progressively smaller nuts, cones and pods is added. A "bow" of okra or honey-locust pods provides a finishing touch for the completed wreath, which is a handsome complement for a large green or brown candle.

XI
CHRISTMAS
IN THE
COLONIES

Long before the seventeenth century, English homes and churches had been decorated with evergreens for the holidays, which extended from Christmas Eve through Twelfth Night (January 6.) This custom began with the Romans, who ornamented houses and temples with greenery during the midwinter Saturnalia. The early Christians adopted the custom and consecrated it by attaching religious symbolism to the pagan wreaths and garlands: evergreens became the symbol of life after death; the wreath, with no end and no beginning, exemplified eternal life; the wreath of holly represented Christ's crown of thorns, and its berries drops of His blood.

Bringing a huge log into the house was a midwinter ritual of tree-worshipping Druids in ancient Britain; the Druids also venerated mistletoe because it seemed miraculous to them that any plant could live high in a tree with no roots in the earth. As the centuries passed, Christian England enjoyed the Yule log and the kissing ball of mistletoe.

Holy Days in the Colonies

In colonial America, Christmas was a season, and not a single day of celebrations, but New England's Pilgrims and Puritans, who were in revolt against the laxity of the Church of England, wanted no part of church-sanctioned pagan customs, and even refused to recognize Christmas Day as a holiday.

The settlers in the Southern Colonies, however, had no quarrel with the English church, and no scruples prevented their enjoyment of the wassail bowl and the Christmas hunt. As long as the Yule log burned, a holiday from all work lasted. They decked the halls with plentiful and beautiful native holly, laurel and ivy, and hung mistletoe in doorways to claim a kiss from any maiden who paused beneath it. For the evergreen oak, rosemary and bay that were also part of England's traditional decorations, they substituted cedar, pine and magnolia. On Christmas Day, there were services in evergreen-decorated churches, and feasting in the homes. Gifts were bestowed on servants and tradespeople, but family members did not exchange presents.

In the New Netherlands, the Dutch began the holiday season on December 6 with the feast of St. Nikolaas, the patron saint of children. Boys and girls set their wooden shoes by the hearth on the eve of this day, and in the morning found them filled with sweetmeats (for the good) or with ashes (for the miscreant). From December 6 to December 25 festivities centered around the dinner table. The portly burghers were great trenchermen, and every *Goede Vrouw* was expected to be a good cook. In Nieuw

Amsterdam, Christmas meant succulent roasts and rich gravies, plump fowl stuffed to the bursting point with oyster dressing, and piping hot doughnuts.

To the French who settled Louisiana, the midnight mass on Christmas Eve was the most solemn religious observance of the year. New Year's Day was the time for joyful celebration, with family feasts and gifts to the children of the household as well as to servants.

New Year's Day Open House

In New England, New Year's Day became a time to keep open house. Since every household followed the custom, each family was divided; some members stayed at home to welcome guests, while others went calling on neighbors and friends. The Middle Colonies had the best of two holiday observances. They shared New England's festive New Year, but they also joined with the South in keeping alive Merrie England's merry Christmas.

Most of America's beloved Christmas customs came to these shores with the settlers from England, Holland and Germany. In the seventeenth century the English had brought to the Southern Colonies the love of holly wreaths, evergreen garlands, and bunches of mistletoe. The Dutch had been accompanied to the New World by their thin, red-robed and mitred St. Nikolaas who was destined to undergo a gradual metamorphosis into chubby, jolly Santa Claus who looked more like a burgher than a bishop.

EIGHTEENTH-CENTURY HOLIDAYS *Christmas Customs*

By 1700, religious dissenters from Germany had settled in Pennsylvania, bringing their own special contributions to American holiday customs: the lighted candle, and the Christmas tree.

In Germany, during the Middle Ages, an especially large candle was lighted in each church at the Christmas Eve Mass, to symbolize the Star of Bethlehem. By degrees, the ceremonial lighting of a Christmas Eve candle became the custom in every home; set in a front window, its light was a greeting to passers-by and an affirmation of faith.

Ceremonial Candles

During the Reformation, Martin Luther himself is said to have decorated the first Christmas tree. Legend has it that as he walked alone among bare-branched trees at the edge of a forest on a cold, clear December night, he was struck by the beauty of a small fir tree bravely testifying by its bright green foliage that life was everlasting. Outlined against the sky, its branches seemed to be tipped with twinkling stars. Martin Luther took the little fir tree home with him as a lesson for his children, placing lighted candles upon its branches to simulate stars. German Protestants quickly adopted the candlelit tree as a special decoration for the Christmas season, and carried the tradition with them when they emigrated to America.

Christmas Tree

In a contemporary account of a public Christmas celebration at Bethlehem, Pennsylvania, in 1747, this statement appears:

> For this occasion several small pyramids and one large pyramid of green brushwood had been prepared, all decorated with candles and the large one with apples . . .

In the homes of Bethlehem, the Moravians who had founded the town trimmed their Christmas trees not only with candles and apples, but also pointed stars of heavy white paper. Women took great pride in their ability to cut, fold, and glue these intricate and charming decorations, and the directions were a closely guarded secret, handed down from mother to daughter to the present day. Moravian paper stars still are made (and sold) in Bethlehem, and at Old Salem in Winston-Salem, North Carolina.

74 and 75.   *In 1776, Moravians founded a well-planned, self-contained community near the center of their hundred-thousand-acre tract in North Carolina, and named the new town Salem, which means Peace. In 1769, the large Brothers' House was built as a home and workshop for the single men of the community; there young men learned trades from master craftsmen, in an atmosphere of moral and spiritual discipline. In the deep cellar of the Brothers' House (now a part of the extensive restoration, Old Salem) the building of the Christmas putz is an annual tradition.*

The scene above is a reproduction of the town of Salem as it appeared during the years 1830 to 1860; the scale of the model is one inch to eight feet. Nestled together against a snowy background, the buildings cluster around The Home Moravian Church, shown at upper left. The Brothers' House, where the putz is on display, is in the right foreground.

In another detail from the model of Old Salem, below, a grist mill is shown, with an arched bridge across the millrace below its movable water wheel. The tiny wagons, animals, cornshucks and men, carved with marvelous precision, are less than one-inch long!

The Christmas tree's ornaments also included thin, spicy cookies that *Moravian Cookies* had been the delight of children in the Moravians' homeland, Bohemia. Housewives brought to Pennsylvania wooden molds for shaping dough into stars, hearts, crescents and animals, and the recipe for the cakes. Translated from the original weights to modern measures (and greatly reduced in volume) it reads:

½ cup brown sugar	1 teaspoon powdered cloves
1 cup dark molasses	1 teaspoon ground ginger
3 tablespoonfuls butter	½ teaspoon mace
3 tablespoonfuls lard	2 teaspoons baking soda
1 tablespoon ground cinnamon	4 cups flour

Add the sugar to the molasses and mix well. Melt the butter and lard together, cool slightly, and stir into the molasses. Sift into this mixture the spices and the soda with one-half cup of the flour. Stir well. Add the remaining flour and knead the dough until thoroughly mixed (it will be exceedingly stiff.) Let the dough ripen in the refrigerator for at least two days. Roll out in small amounts on a well-floured surface, *to a thickness of no more than one-sixteenth inch.* Cut in star, heart, crescent, fluted circle, and animal shapes. Bake on greased cookie sheets at 375°F. for about ten minutes; tops should not brown. The six dozen delicious paper-thin cookies will keep for weeks in an air-tight tin, or for months in the freezer.

In the first Massachusetts and Virginia settlements, popcorn was an *Popcorn Chains* astonishment and a joy to adults and children alike. Several slender ears were kept hanging on the kitchen wall, and served as decorations until such time as their pointed yellow grains were put in a covered kettle and popped over the open fire. The colonists ate popcorn plain, as did the Indians; they also found it delicious served with milk, and it was the old-original dry breakfast cereal. When hot boiled molasses was poured over the fluffy grains, the resultant sticky mass could be molded between buttered palms into balls that hardened to crisp candy. Popcorn balls became a traditional sweet. Heaped in a bowl, they both decorated a dinner table and provided dessert. In the Middle Colonies and the South, Christmas was not complete without them.

Then some experimenter found that the popped kernels could be pierced with a needle and strung on thread. Chains of popcorn were used throughout the year on festive occasions.

The first German Lutherans in Pennsylvania were as amazed and delighted by popcorn as the earliest English settlers had been. When Christmas came, they draped snowy popcorn chains from branch to branch of an evergreen tree, and thus created the first American contribution to Christmas decorations.

Underneath the Christmas tree, German families placed a *putz* (from *The Putz* the word *putzen,* meaning "to decorate"). According to legend, the first nativity scene had been assembled by St. Francis of Assisi, and crèches had been used for centuries in the Churches of Italy, France, and Middle Europe. Miniature tabletop manger scenes, with hand-carved wooden shepherds, Wise Men, and domestic animals surrounding the Holy Family, were made for home use. They were cherished possessions, brought out for each holiday season, and added to from year to year. In Germanic principalities, other carved miniatures—houses, carts, men and women in con-

76. *The Christmas tree was introduced to America by Germans who settled in Pennsylvania in the early eighteenth century. The first tree decorations, dating from the time of Martin Luther, had been candles. Red apples, thin spicy shaped cookies, and paper stars with twenty-four slender points had come to be traditional; the popcorn chain was America's own contribution to Christmas decorations. Before 1850, imported German tree ornaments were large, heavy balls and bunches of grapes, made of molded glass. Beside the short, hand-dipped candle is a holder of scalloped tin, to be clipped to a tree branch.*

temporary dress—began to be added to the Christmas display; in time these secular representations were separated from the religious scene, and placed beneath the tree.

In the German settlements of colonial Pennsylvania, the "Christmas yard" was a family project. Father and sons carved and whittled animals, buildings, trees, and people, and perhaps such a curiosity as a minute mill with a movable water wheel. Mother and daughters dressed the human figures in scraps of cloth, and painted the other miniatures. The whole family joined in setting up the putz beneath the tree on Christmas Eve—a snowy landscape (a linen sheet strewn with wisps of white wool) with a mirrored frozen pond for tiny skaters, or a barnyard complete in every detail.

Gingerbread Cookies   While German children in Pennsylvania were hanging thin ginger cookies on the Christmas tree, the children of English settlers were enjoying gingerbread. Squares of "Muster Day gingerbread," a thin hard-glazed variety, were sold at public gatherings and fairs; when made for home consumption, it could be shaped with a knife before baking into animals, birds, or human figures. Gingerbread boys (or girls) were given to children as rewards; as an extra luxury, raisins were pressed into the uncooked dough to form eyes, nose, mouth, and buttons. Sweet-cakes did not come a child's way very often. They were carried about and played with until they began to crumble, and only then were they eaten. Extra large gingerbread shapes were made for children as a Christmas treat, sometimes British soldiers with coats of red sugar, or houses with snowy roofs of white icing. By the middle of the eighteenth century, tinsmiths were selling cutters for gingerbread, and it was no longer necessary for cooks to be artists in order to make such figures.

Evergreen Branches

In the Middle Colonies and the South, the English colonists were elaborating on the holly wreaths and pine garlands of earlier days. A plain green wreath hung at each front window of town houses. Dried materials (small sprays of wheat, red leaves, celosia, and lunaria) were combined with evergreens in wreaths for overmantels. Garlands of pine were swagged over doorways and up stairway banisters, and caught up with red ribbons and clusters of slender white-pine cones. Mantels were banked with holly, spruce, and pine, with bunches of red oak leaves tucked in for added color. Sprays of holly were wedged behind the frames of mirrors and of pictures.

Kissing Balls

At first, a kissing ball had been only a large round bunch of mistletoe on a single stem, suspended from a nail in the center of a doorway. By the mid-eighteenth century, a spherical shape seemed all-important; twigs of mistletoe were tied together around wet moss, and bound with crossed ribbons. The ribbons, tied at the top, provided a convenient means of attaching the ball to a chandelier.

Now that mistletoe has become an expensive rarity, kissing balls usually are made of other small-leafed greenery, with a few small sprigs of mistletoe to satisfy convention. Chicken wire is molded around a core of soaked Oasis or wet sphagnum moss. Twigs of boxwood, azalea, or round-leafed holly are inserted through the wire mesh into the moist center, and keep fresh for several days. Mistletoe is added, and a ribbon (threaded through the mesh at the top of the ball and knotted for security) supplies the hanger.

Fruit Decorations

Fresh fruit was the favorite Christmas decoration throughout the eighteenth century, and at this season the best of the carefully preserved apples, pears, melons, grapes and pomegranates were brought forth to be heaped in bowls and compotes or epergnes. Ripe pomegranates spoiled rapidly when relegated to the root cellar with apples and pears, and shrivelled when placed like fresh grapes in wood ashes, but they were so much a part of English holiday tradition that the colonists were determined to find a way of keeping them. The solution was to dry them, like gourds, by piercing them at both ends and placing them on paper in a dim loft, turning and wiping them every day. Dried pomegranates were a little less brilliant in color and had slightly wrinkled skins, but they were infinitely better than no pomegranates at all. The indispensible punchbowl on a side table in the dining room rested in a nest of holly garnished with lemons, apples, and almonds.

della Robbia Wreaths and Garlands

The fruit-embellished terra cotta wreaths and garlands of the fifteenth-century sculptor, Luca della Robbia, were much admired in eighteenth-century Europe, and widely copied there and in America in living materials. Apples, lemons, oranges, nuts and cones were added to evergreen wreaths and to garlands laid flat on a table.

For door, wall, or mantel decorations, della Robbia wreaths are made by wiring fruits, nuts, and cones to ready-made wreaths of fresh pine, spruce, or boxwood twigs. Focal areas of fruit are established first, and smaller fruits fill in the full, irregular circle.

Since in the eighteenth century it was customary to lay such a wreath flat on a table and to make it very large, it is easier to reproduce the effect of that period with no framework at all. Short sprays of foliage, all pointing in the same direction, are overlapped so that the stem of one is tucked under and hidden by the leaves or needles of the next. Fruits, nuts and cones, in colorful groupings, are simply laid in place. Apples and pears are almost invariably included for their attractive colors and shapes; crab-apples and seckel pears are more nearly similar in size to those actually available in the colonial period. Lemons, limes and small oranges would be historically correct, since they were brought regularly from the West Indies, and pomegranates, prominently placed. Small bunches of fresh grapes or raisins would be appropriate for a table wreath; half pineapples make large and showy focal points, but would have been available only near the seacoast. All the native varieties of nuts, in their shells—hickory, hazel, black walnut, and chestnut— would be correct, plus almonds which were imported very early because they had so long been considered the proper ending for any feast. Long and slender white-pine cones provide a very useful change of shape, particularly for the outside edge of such a wreath. Clusters of small hemlock "roses" are excellent fillers, as are sprigs of holly or bittersweet berries.

The garlands of fruit that extended the length of a table are similarly made. A length of pine or laurel roping from the florist is a helpful starting point but not a necessity; sprays of foliage may simply be laid flat on the table. Beginning at the center, all the sprigs should be faced toward the ends of the table; the garland may be straight, or gently S-curved. Fruits, nuts, cones and berry clusters are laid on top of the garland, informally clustered for best effect, with bridges of plain greenery between the groupings and at each end. In the center of the table, where the exposed stems meet, a mound of fruit surrounded by a flat circle of green leaves provides a neat finish.

Fruit Pyramids   A pyramid of apples was an especially well-loved Christmas table decoration, and one that was equally appropriate for a governor's palace or a modest home. At Colonial Williamsburg, where the apple pyramid is a yearly feature of the elaborate and beautiful Christmas decorations, such an arrangement is made on a flat-topped wooden cone studded with rows of headless finishing nails. An apple is impaled on each spike, and the pyramid is usually topped with a fresh pineapple; short sprays of greenery between and behind the fruits conceal the wooden base completely. (Similar wooden cones are for sale in the Restoration's shops.)

It is highly unlikely that the average colonial household possessed such a spiked cone, nor was one needed. It was perfectly possible to make apple pyramids on a base of cabbages. A large, flat head (trimmed at the bottom if necessary to stand steady) formed the base of the cone, a smaller and more spherical head the middle portion, and half a small round cabbage was the top. A dowel stick (it might have been a long wooden knitting

77. *No decoration was more universally loved and used than the apple pyramid that combined red polished fruit and fresh evergreens in the traditional Christmas colors. Here boxwood twigs provide the background for small lady apples turned to show their blossom ends. A tuft of pineapple foliage tops the cone; using the leaves after the fruit had been eaten was a favorite "deceit" of the eighteenth century. The fruit arrangement is surrounded by a wreath of boxwood twigs. Pyramids were made on wooden cones studded with finishing nails, or on stacked cabbageheads. This one is shown in the keeping room of the Adam Thoroughgood House, owned by the City of Norfolk, Virginia.*

78. *Colonial Williamsburg's outstanding Christmas decorations are an integral part of the holiday festivities that attract visitors from every section of America. The overmantel of the family dining room in the Governor's Palace is simply but effectively adorned with four small wreaths of boxwood twigs and sprays of bayberry. On the mantel, below the portrait of Governor Alexander Spotswood, bright-red apples and dark-green magnolia leaves emphasize the traditional Christmas colors.*

needle) was pressed down through all three layers to hold them together securely. Apples on short sharpened sticks were stuck into the cabbages; beginning at the bottom, the heads were covered with row after row of touching fruits. Then short sprays of pine or hemlock were placed between the rows of apples, and the humble basis of the cone was completely concealed. Such pyramids were dormants—used as decoration but intended to be eaten eventually. When the apples were gone, the cabbages were removed from the dowel stick and went unharmed into the cooking pot.

In Holland, fruit pyramids had been made on plates of graduated sizes; a round platter was covered with large apples; around its rim, they were laid on their sides with the stems facing out. A smaller plate was balanced on top of the fruit, and filled with smaller apples. A third very small plate or saucer was added, holding three small apples laid on their sides and topped with a large apple right side up. Early Dutch settlers made these tiered table ornaments with Delft plates, not only at Christmas but throughout the year on festive occasions. When the pyramids were copied, in the eighteenth century, in neighboring colonies, pewter or Chinese porcelain plates were more often used.

In the late 1700's, tiered fruit stands—ceramic, glass, or silver—replaced the balanced plates and produced the same sort of pyramidal arrangement.

After 1800, when the Classic Revival reached the United States, wreaths and garlands became thin and slendor. Flat feathery hemlock wreaths were preferred to bushy ones of holly, and laurel roping replaced garlands of white pine.

NINETEENTH CENTURY

Nuts and Cones

Grinling Gibbons' carved wooden fruits, nuts, berries, pods and cones combined in Classic style served as the models for wreaths and swags at Christmas time. Wreaths had as their backing narrow circlets of metal; garlands were sometimes made on thin wooden shapes, with holes bored for convenient wiring on of fruit. For wreaths, fruits were pierced with long wires that were wrapped around the metal frame and twisted together at the back. Cones, with wires inserted between the two lowest rows of scales, were also wired in place. Nuts presented a greater problem. Holes had to be hammered through the harder shells with an awl; the thinner varieties could be pierced with a heated wire. Often it seemed simpler to glue the nuts together in clusters, and to glue each cluster to the frame.

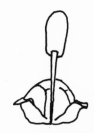

With the exception of the very popular dried pomegranates, the fruits were highly perishable; the other materials, however, were well nigh indestructible. Soon wreaths and swags were being made without fruit, using only nuts, pods, and cones. It was easier to glue these materials to a wooden backing than to wire them on, and here were permanent decorations that could be put away until the next holiday season or left in place the year around. The completed composition usually was given a protective coat of shellac or varnish that added a desirable sheen, but the all-brown wreaths and garlands still seemed dull and lifeless. Gilding some of the nuts and pods before gluing them to the frame added a certain distinction, and when the edges of some cones were touched with gold, the composition was greatly enlivened. In the French Empire manner, both wreaths and garlands were further embellished with spirals of narrow, pastel ribbon, and the effect was restrained and very elegant.

79. *As the frontier moved westward during the nineteenth century, Christmas decorations in pioneer outposts were necessarily primitive, like this wall ornament of pinecones, light-tan cotton pods, mahogany-colored honey-locust pods, and yellow martingourd. The "pretties" are strung on a leather thong. The decoration is from the Craft Center, Gatlinburg, Tennessee.*

Pyramids of pine cones, pods, and nuts could be made on the same sort of plaster cones that held shell flowers. A dab of fresh plaster bonded the individual additions to the central core.

Cone and nut decorations remained in use at holiday time throughout the Victorian period, especially in the Southwest where piñon cones and nuts became a new Christmas tradition, and on the northern Pacific Coast, where gigantic sugar-pine cones were a decoration in themselves.

Returning to the original Grinling Gibbons' carvings for inspiration, North Carolina mountain women now make elegant and lacy wreaths on wire frames, and incorporate a single pea-pod in each. An outstanding feature of the composition is the bunch of grapes that is in reality a cluster of pecans. The nuts are bored with an electric drill, and wired individually; then their wire stems are wrapped together in tight clumps or graceful, graduated bunches. Curved garlands and symmetrical swags, pyramidal potted trees and half-round tree-shaped door hangings feature large round sliced cones along with whole slim white-pine fingers. Candlesticks, candelabra, and wall sconces are decked with light and airy sprays of acorns, pods, and tiny hemlock cones. (These decorations are sold at the Biltmore Country Market, in Asheville.)

Christmas Trees in the Nineteenth Century

During the Revolutionary War, homesick Hessian soldiers celebrated Christmas in New Jersey and the Hudson River Valley by erecting Christmas trees. The Dutch residents of these areas took careful note; after the bitterness of the war was over, they began to trim trees for their own children. They were accustomed to using eggs as decorations—America's first colored Easter eggs had been rolled at Fort Orange (Albany) very early in the seventeenth century—so they made delicate and beautiful ornaments of blown shells, cutting a window in one side and arranging a tiny scene within. Gilded nuts were suspended from the branches; ring-shaped cookies were slipped over the tips of twigs, for the children to remove and eat.

Before 1800, the grandsons of Pennsylvania's early German settlers were migrating southward in search of more land. Christmas trees were set up and decorated in Virginia, North Carolina, South Carolina, Kentucky and Tennessee, to the amazement of Anglo-Saxon neighbors and to the envy of their children. Southerners had always made much of Christmas, and they recognized in the Christmas tree a valuable addition to their accepted notions of greenery in the home. Between 1830 and 1850, the custom of trimming a small tree became widespread.

Wherever Germans went, they took along their cooking and their customs. Down the Ohio to Cincinnati, north to Milwaukee, down the Mississippi to St. Louis, on to Kansas and Nebraska went the thrifty farmers and artisans. Come Christmas, a tall tree was brought in and trimmed with candles, apples, horns, paper chains and cutouts, cookies, and strings of popcorn. By this time, in Germany, heavy ornaments of molded glass were being made, and a few began to be imported. Fortunate families hung one or two huge shining balls in prominent spots on the tree.

Christmas Stockings and Other Treats for Children

The ancient Dutch custom of setting out the children's shoes in anticipation of a visit from St. Nikolaas had been altered to the hanging of stockings from the mantel on Christmas Eve. Clement Clarke Moore described how

The stockings were hung by the chimney with care
In hopes that St. Nicholas soon would be there . . .

A Visit from St. Nicholas was first published in a Troy, New York, newspaper in 1823; its popularity was to make the Christmas stocking the universal perquisite of American childhood.

In 1835, southern-born President Andrew Jackson had the White House decorated with holly and mistletoe, and hung the stockings of his grandchildren from the mantel in his own bedroom to be sure of sharing their excitement on Christmas morning. Following southern custom, each stocking no doubt contained sugarplums and roasted goober peas (peanuts), tin horns and wooden whistles, and a coin or a toy tucked into the toe. There may have been a "walking cane" protruding from the top.

Molasses taffy was a favorite sweet, and children were allowed to have taffy-pulls as part of holiday celebrations. The bubbling brown syrup was poured out to cool on a marble slab; when it could be handled with buttered

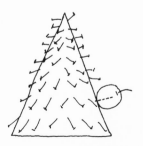

80. *In the South, where transplanted English holiday customs had taken root early in colonial days, the Christmas tree came into use in the second quarter of the nineteenth century. The gracious Low House was built in Savannah, Georgia, in 1848; here Juliette Gordon Low organized the first Girl Scout troop in America in 1912. Since 1928, this has been the headquarters of the Georgia chapter of the National Society of the Colonial Dames of America. The doorway between its double drawing rooms is garlanded with boxwood and longleaf pine; hanging from a red velvet bow in the center, a kissing ball of boxwood sprigs is finished with a spray of mistletoe. The tall pier glass and the portrait are outlined with pine roping, and the mantel is centered with a bowl of evergreens and cones. Focal point of the decoration is the table tree in the corner, trimmed in the American Victorian manner with strings of popcorn, popcorn balls, cookies, candy canes, paper cutouts, and baskets or cornucopias of hard candies. Wrapped packages and toys are grouped below it.*

fingers, it was pulled until it turned silvery white. Just before it hardened, it could be cut with scissors into short lengths and one end of each stick could be knobbed or curved into a handle. Then it became customary to cook the syrup in two small batches, leaving one plain, but coloring and flavoring the other with cherry juice. The two batches were pulled into very slender strings and twisted together in a spiral, and the red-and-white candy cane had arrived.

Long since, along the northeastern seaboard, the cranberries that grew *New England Celebrations* in such profusion had been teamed with turkey for Thanksgiving repasts. While dormants still were in use, a skinned and roasted bird sometimes was returned to its plumage and given a cranberry necklace. Strings of bright red cranberries quite naturally found a place on the Christmas tree in the Middle Colonies (where in Pennsylvania the tree had first been introduced), a fine foil for chains of white popcorn.

Meanwhile, in New England, the joys of Christmas had overcome the lingering interdiction of Puritan conscience. Christmas feasts rivalled Thanksgiving dinners in opulence. Bowls of holly and polished red apples stood about on tables; garlands of greenery outlined doorways, mantels, mirrors, and family portraits. On Boston's Beacon Hill, a lighted candle in each front window on Christmas Eve recalled the Illuminations of the colonial period. An orange (still a great luxury in the days before rapid, refrigerated transport) was the special surprise tucked into the toe of each Christmas stocking that bulged with candies and small mementoes. Christmas trees, however, were very few in number.

In England, the Christmas tree had no part in holiday decorations until 1841, when Prince Albert had one erected at Windsor Castle for the infant *The Christmas Tree* Prince of Wales. By 1842, the Court was following the lead of the royal *Comes of Age* family, and trees appeared in stately homes; by mid-century, they were to be seen in city houses and country cottages.

In 1850, the December issue of *Godey's Lady's Book* treated the American public to a picture of the 1847 table tree at Windsor Castle, with the royal family grouped around it. Its branches were laden with fragile blown-glass ornaments from Germany, on narrow velvet ribbons, and tipped with candles; a waxen angel with outspread wings was attached to the topmost twig. Queen Victoria was greatly admired and respected in the erstwhile American colonies, especially in New England. Since she had publicly set her seal of approval on the Chrismas tree, it suddenly was almost obligatory to have one. Canny New Englanders, however, looked askance at lighted candles on a highly flammable cedar or pine sapling, and often left them off entirely. If they did attach the scalloped tin holders to the branch tips, the candles were lighted only briefly, on Christmas morning, to delight the children while adults stood by with pails of water and buckets of sand. Blown-glass ornaments from Germany, shiny and small, were so carefully packed away in cotton that some have survived through several generations. Tiny tin tops and china penny-dolls were tied to twigs with narrow red velvet or satin ribbon; small wrapped packages dangled from sturdier branches. Cornucopias of shiny paper held satiny "pillows" of hard candy. Confectioners were making red and white peppermint sticks and candy canes, and these found their way into the stockings and onto the tree.

In 1889, Mrs. Benjamin Harrison ordered the first Christmas tree for the White House, and dignified President Harrison was so delighted that he took time off from affairs of state to help the staff with its trimming. Mrs. Harrison was an arbiter of taste, and the news of the White House tree dispelled the last vestiges of doubt that it was proper to have one. In Portland, Maine, and Portland, Oregon, in New Jersey and New Mexico, evergreen trees put forth miraculous fruits on Christmas Eve.

Crafts and customs had always changed when they were transported from the Old World to the New. Decorating for Christmas combined and altered diverse elements into a composite whole that was greater than the sum of its parts, and typically American.

81.   *Following a custom made popular by St. Francis of Assisi, Nativity scenes have been made of many different materials in all parts of the world. Unusual, but reverent in feeling, is this group, made entirely of natural-colored cornshucks by a member of the Southern Highland Handicraft Guild. Each face has painted features; hair and beards of cornsilk have been glued in place. The standing figures are twelve-inches tall.*

LIST OF ILLUSTRATIONS

Black and White

Color
(between pages 96 and 97)

SELECTED BIBLIOGRAPHY

Anders, Nedda C. *Appliqué Old and New*. New York: Hearthside Press, 1967.

Baker, Muriel L. *A Handbook of American Crewel Embroidery*. Rutland: Charles E. Tuttle Co., 1966.

Barnett, James H. *The American Christmas*. New York: The Macmillan Company, 1954.

Bauer, John E. *Christmas on the American Frontier*. Caldwell: Caxton Printers, Ltd., 1961.

Birrell, Verla. *The Textile Arts*. New York: Harper and Brothers, 1959.

Christie, Mrs. Archibald. *Samplers and Stitches*. New York: Hearthside Press, 1959.

Comstock, Helen. *American Furniture*. New York: Viking Press, 1962.

Earle, Alice Morse. *Home Life In Colonial Days*. New York: The Macmillan Company, (1898) 1954.

Eaton, Allen H. *Handicrafts of New England*. New York: Harper and Brothers, 1949.

Eberlein, Harold D. and McClure, Abbot. *The Practical Book of American Antiques Exclusive of Furniture*. Garden City: Garden City Publishing Company, 1927.

Finch, Elfreda. *Flowers and Furniture in America's Historic Homes*. New York: Hearthside Press, 1967.

Fisher, Louise B. *An Eighteenth Century Garland*. Williamsburg: Colonial Williamsburg, Inc., 1951.

Gannon, Ruth. *Winter Bouquets With Color*. New York: Thomas Y. Crowell Company, 1951.

Gratz, George. *The Furniture Doctor*. Garden City: Doubleday and Company, 1962.

Harrower, Dorothy. *Decoupage, A Limitless World in Decoration*. New York: M. Barrows and Company, 1958.

Hillier, Mary. *Pageant of Toys*. New York: Taplinger Publishing Company, Inc., 1966.

Hinson, Dolores A. *Quilting Manual*. New York: Hearthside Press, 1966.

Holliday, Carl. *Woman's Life in Colonial Days*. New York: Frederick Ungar Publishing Company, (1922) 1960.

Ickis, Marguerite. *Folk Arts and Crafts*. New York: Association Press, 1958.

Jeffrey, Tina C. and Jones, Claude, Jr. *Williamsburg Christmas Decorations*. Williamsburg: The Virginia Gazette, 1967.

Krauss, Helen K. *Shell Art*. New York: Hearthside Press, 1965.

Lathrop, Elise. *Historic Houses of Early America*. New York: Robert M. McBride and Company, 1927.

Lewis, Griselda. *Handbook of Crafts*. Newton: Charles T. Branford Company, 1960.

Marcus, Margaret Fairbanks. *Period Flower Arrangement*. New York: M. Barrows and Company, 1952.

McClinton, Katharine Morrison. *Collecting American Victorian Antiques*. New York: Charles Scribner's Sons, 1966.

Nicholson, Arnold. *American Houses in History*. New York: Viking Press, 1965.

Ormsbee, Thomas H. *Collecting Antiques in America*. New York: Hearthside Press, 1962.

Rogers, Meyric R., editor. *American Rooms in Miniature*. Chicago: The Art Institute of Chicago, 1941.

Ravenal, Harriott Horry. *Eliza Pinckney*. New York: Charles Scribner's Sons, 1896.

Savage, George. *A Concise History of Interior Decoration.* London: Thames and Hudson, 1966.

Shanklin, Margaret Eberhardt. *Use of Native Craft Materials.* Peoria: Manual Arts Press, 1947.

Speare, Elizabeth George. *Life in Colonial America.* New York: Random House, 1963.

Taylor, Doris W. and Hart, Anne Button. *China Painting.* Princeton: D. Van Nostrand Company, 1962.

Thompson, Dorothea S. *Creative Decorations With Dried Flowers.* New York: Hearthside Press, 1965.

Tunis, Edwin. *Colonial Living.* Cleveland: World Publishing Company, 1957.

Tunis, Edwin. *Frontier Living.* Cleveland: World Publishing Company, 1961.

Wardlaw, Georgia Dickinson. *The Old and the Quaint in Virginia.* Richmond: Dietz Press, 1939.

Wilson, Nadine Cox. *A Guide to Decoration in the Early American Manner.* Newton: Charles T. Branford Company, 1960.

Winchester, Alice. *The Antiques Treasury.* New York: E. P. Dutton, 1959.

INDEX   185